SPOTLIGHT

W9-DBO-498

WITHDRAWN

SAN DIEGO COUNTY BEACHES

ALAN BISBORT & PARKE PUTERBAUGH

Contents

How to Use This Book

Beaches are identified with numbers, which correspond to the numbers on the map.

Write-ups of each community or locale open with a general essay describing its physical look and layout, attractions and activities, history and sociology, and anything else that might enhance a useful overview. We've also supplied contact information for local chambers of commerce, convention and visitors bureaus, and tourist development councils.

Additional information follows under the following headings: Beaches, Recreation and Attractions, Accommodations, Coastal Cuisine, and Nightlife.

BEACHES

We offer the lowdown on what you can expect to see and do at every publicly accessible beach. This includes a description of a beach's natural features and any other relevant observations. Each beach also has its own "beach profile": a listing of practical information, including directions, activities, parking and day-use fees, hours, facilities, and contact number. A **BEST** symbol also accompanies the profiles of best beaches.

Each beach profile also includes symbols for certain activities beyond the beach basics of swimming and sunbathing. Since one can go fishing on virtually any beach, we haven't included a special fishing symbol. However, our jetty and pier symbols indicate when those particular angling opportunities are available. The activity symbols are as follows:

Biking/jogging

Camping (developed campground or campgrounds)

Diving/snorkeling (popular spot for diving and/or snorkeling)

Hiking (trail or trails for nature observation and/or exercise)

Jetty (rock structure extending seaward from the mouth of an inlet or harbor, making for good fishing, snorkeling, and surfing)

Pier (wooden or concrete structure from which people fish or stroll)

Surfing (sufficiently sizable and well-formed waves that draw more than the occasional surfer)

Volleyball (volleyball nets and standards on the beach or park grounds)

Nude beach (clothing optional)

We've also included information on facilities available at each beach:
- Concession (food and drink available at or near beach)
- Lifeguards (year-round, unless identified as "seasonal")
- Picnic area
- Restrooms
- Showers
- Visitors center (staffed facility with information and exhibits)

RECREATION AND ATTRACTIONS

This selective listing is a kind of quick-and-dirty Yellow Pages that we've compiled for selected communities.
- Bike/Skate Rentals (bicycles, in-line skates, and other fun stuff)
- Boat Cruise (sightseeing trips on the water)
- Dive Shop (diving equipment and/or dive trips)
- Ecotourism (canoe/kayak outfitter or site for ecotourist outing)
- Fishing Charters (guided fishing trips)
- Horseback Riding
- Lighthouse
- Marina (boat dockage)
- Pier
- Rainy Day Attraction (something to do indoors when the weather is inclement)
- Shopping/Browsing (shopping district, center, or mall of note)
- Sportfishing
- Surf Report (surf forecast)
- Surf Shop (surfboards and surf gear)
- Vacation Rentals (beach houses and/or condos for short-term rental)

ACCOMMODATIONS

We offer a general overview of lodging options, as well as brief descriptions of selected hotels, motels, and resorts we'd recommend when planning a beach vacation. Our write-ups are based on actual stays and site visits. Because room rates fluctuate, we provide general guidelines of price range. Our $–$$$$ symbols are offered as general indicators of the nightly charge in season for a standard room with two beds.

$ = inexpensive (under $80 per night)

$$ = moderate ($80–129)

$$$ = moderately expensive ($130–179)

$$$$ = expensive ($180 and up)

COASTAL CUISINE

We offer a general overview of the dining scene, as well as descriptive write-ups of restaurants specializing in seafood and/or regional cuisine that are located on or near the beach. We cast a favorable eye upon places that have been around a while and have maintained a reputation for consistency and quality. Our $–$$$$ symbols are general indicators that reflect the median cost of an à la carte dinner entrée.

$ = inexpensive ($10 and under)

$$ = moderate ($11–17)

$$$ = moderately expensive ($18–24)

$$$$ = expensive ($25 and up)

NIGHTLIFE

Our concept of nightlife is people gathering to relax or blow off steam after the sun sets. Our listings run the gamut from tiki bars and coffeehouses to clubs with live music or deejays—in other words, anywhere you can kick back and have fun during and after sunset. We've made the rounds, looking for the liveliest good times. And we let you know when you're better off not wasting your time.

MAP SYMBOLS

Expressway	⑧⓪ Interstate Freeway	✗ Airfield
Primary Road	⑩①① U.S. Highway	✈ Airport
Secondary Road	㉑ State Highway	○ City/Town
Unpaved Road	66 County Highway	▲ Mountain
Ferry	Lake	▲ Park
National Border	Dry Lake	)(Pass
State Border	Seasonal Lake	◉ State Capital

SAN DIEGO COUNTY BEACHES

The United States could not have rolled out a more inviting welcome mat on its southwest border than the beaches of San Diego County. They extend for 76 miles, from the wide-open party towns of Ocean Beach, Mission Beach, and Pacific Beach to the upscale, uphill village of La Jolla, and from the rugged setting of Torrey Pines State Beach to the discreet charms of north county communities like Del Mar and Carlsbad. Admittedly, it all ends with a thud at the military city of Oceanside and the nuclear reactors at San Onofre. But the many miles of this state-sized county cover a broad range of settings: lengthy stretches of soft sand; thin, silvery strands of hard-packed sand; cobble-covered beaches that have lost their sand; and rocky coves, sea caves, and sandstone cliffs. There are also bays, lagoons, estuaries, and underwater reserves.

There is beach erosion as well—a recurring problem that has necessitated large-scale "beach renourishment" projects along various thinning parts of the coast. The future of such costly interventions is seriously in doubt, and some coastal scientists believe the best policy is strategic retreat. What we have witnessed over the past quarter century in all parts of San Diego County resembles the ordeal of Sisyphus: the beach erodes, the beach is widened, the beach erodes again, and the cycle repeats ad infinitum. From one end of San Diego County to the other, on beach after beach, studies conducted in this decade all come to the same conclusion: "Ongoing beach and seacliff erosion threatens public and private development, as well as public safety." These drumbeats calling for continual renourishment have become as repetitive as a mantra. And continuing to throw money at vanishing sand has become increasingly hard to rationalize for those who are not kept busy by such projects.

San Diego's varied coastal locales play host

© PARKE PUTERBAUGH

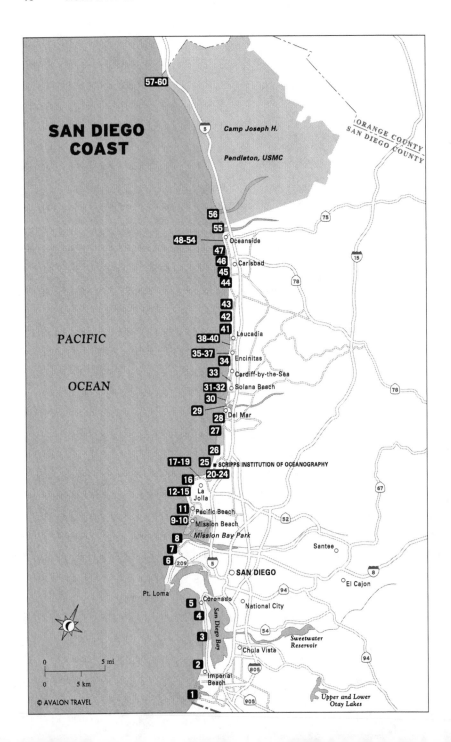

to every manner of activity that beach lovers live to indulge in: surfing, swimming, sailing, sunbathing, biking, fishing, camping, volleyball, and ogling one another. Then there are the post-sundown activities in these mostly revved-up beach towns: beer drinking, taco scarfing, partying, flirting, hanging out…you get the idea. In short, San Diego County is the apotheosis of the beach life. Its communities offer the quintessential Southern California beach experience.

This was brought home to us on a recent Fourth of July. At midnight, on some inexplicable impulse, we found ourselves wandering out to Windansea Beach in La Jolla. The surfers were off partying at their favorite dive bars and overcrowded apartments, but the waves continued to roar. We sat on a stony ledge, inhaling huge drafts of salt-sprayed air while staring at the dark, endlessly churning sea. It could have been the setting for everything from *The Endless Summer* to more '60s flicks than you could shake a beach blanket at. Whoosh, splash, boom, roar. This short detour to Windansea Beach invigorated us for days thereafter, like a contact high with a vast oceanic fountain of youth.

Border Field State Park

We tend to spill more words on Border Field than this godforsaken place merits because it's where California begins and is therefore where our coastal treks begin as well. It is a fascinating place for a variety of reasons, none

of which has much to do with beaches. So if you want to skip this epistle about a crumbling state park in the middle of nowhere, you won't hurt our feelings. But if you are into the symbolism of starting points, then Border Field must be visited. Just be careful if you come out here.

Border Field sits on the California-Mexico border and serves as a favorite point of entry for illegal aliens. They either scale the rusty 10-foot fence that separates the United States from Mexico—at least until the more impregnable wall that's under construction is completed—or brazenly wade out at low tide

© PARKE PUTERBAUGH

Border Field State Park

ON THE BORDER

All the issues that plague California have been compressed onto the beaches near the Mexican border. You name it, they've got it: illegal immigration, sewage disposal, farm runoff, ocean contamination, shoddy development, flooding, erosion, vandalism, overpopulation, litter.

We learned this on our first visit to Border Field State Park and the Tijuana River Estuary back in 1988. The trip started out promisingly, with green, irrigated sod fields bordering Dairy Mart and Monument Roads and rugged, dry hills in the distance. It did not take long for things to turn nasty.

Hand-lettered signs sprang up on the side of Monument Road as we headed toward the ocean. One announced: Environmentalists Destroy Human Lives. Another trumpeted: Welcome to No Man's Land. Environmentalists. Illegal Aliens. Smuggling. Flooding. Sewage. Garbage. A series of signs blamed environmentalists for hurting the economy, for "desperate animals caught in the mud," and for the drownings of 24 illegals. At the bottom of one such sign were spray-painted the ominous words: Remember Waco, Texas.

On the Mexican side, shoddily built villas could be seen dotting the dry brown hillsides, some clinging precariously to their high perches, which are now illuminated at night by powerful mobile floodlights. Border Patrol minivans could also be seen, secreted behind clumps of dry weeds and dirt. Like enormous metal insects, the feds' paddy wagons lie in wait for fence-hoppers who might try their luck inland from the more popular Border Field State Park. This entire end of the U.S.-Mexico boundary is the most sieve-like in the country, accounting for nearly one-third of all illegal alien arrests. As many as 80,000 arrests have been made in the peak months of April and May, when seasonal employment lures migrant workers.

Things did not improve at the beach. The state park ranger who took our fare was as beat as the scene around him. "Do you ever get busy at the park?" we asked, cheerful naïfs that we are.

"We used to," he said, ever so slowly, "but not no more."

Then he sighed and, as if cutting off further questions, said, "It's a long story.... It has nothing to do with the park."

Indeed, the parkland seemed a splendid setting. Then we pulled into a parking lot filled with vehicles sporting Mexican license plates or no plates at all. One group of Mexicans in cowboy hats had disassembled a car, leaving engine parts strewn about the asphalt. They seemed in no hurry to reassemble it.

Mexican radio stations blared from every direction like a musical EKG. Families ate food from plastic bags, bickered and laughed, and fell asleep on the grass and walls. Screaming kids were running everywhere. None, curiously, ventured down to the ocean, where the waves seemed much more enticing than the hot asphalt.

and walk around it into the United States, as if beachcombing.

For those who visit Border Field legally, this makes for an intriguing sociological study but a bummer of a beach trip. Some might argue that only sadists would go out of their way to visit Border Field State Park. Think of us what you will, but we've made a perverse ritual out of beginning every trip up the California coast

here at Border Field. On our visit for the previous edition, torrential rains had nearly washed out the final leg of the rutted dirt road that leads to the parking area on the bluff above the beach. We could see the cement monument that marks the international boundary and the bullfight ring of Tijuana just beyond it, but we could not get up to them. Wary of miring a rental car in this muddy impasse, we

Pregnant women fanned themselves with the lids of take-out fried-chicken buckets. One young couple groped passionately in the grass while an infant lay napping beside their intertwined bodies.

We asked one of the friendly tykes why he wasn't playing in the ocean.

"I used to but not no more."

"Why? Too cold?" No answer. "Smell bad?"

Big smile and a nod.

The ocean waters for several miles north of the border smell bad most of the time. The Mexican sewage treatment plants can't keep up with the load from the burgeoning population, and when the system breaks down, raw sewage flows into the surrounding Tijuana River Estuary and, ultimately, into the ocean. This creates what the Mexicans call *aguas negras* (black waters) – as many as 20 million gallons of it in a single day, which necessitates the closing of beaches as far as 50 miles away by San Diego health officials.

The sewage issue is one for which the United States has been no less culpable than Mexico. In 1999, a much-needed treatment facility – the International Wastewater Treatment Plant – began pumping partially treated sewage from Tijuana into the ocean via an outfall off Imperial Beach. On the American side, a new complex – the South Bay Water Reclamation Project – was up and running in 2002. Fully online now, it treats up to 15 million gallons of sewage a day from the communities of San Ysidro, Chula Vista, and Imperial Beach. Nonetheless, in May 2008, as the summer season was starting, the beaches of Imperial Beach were closed to swimming due to sewage spills. Likewise, it goes without saying that Border Field State Park had barred swimming. The most frequent signs seen on beaches of southernmost San Diego County read: Keep Out. Sewage Contaminated Water. Exposure May Cause Illness.

As if tempting the fecal finger of fate further, "planned communities" are being built right up to the Mexican border. On the Mexican side, a "bi-national" border sewage treatment plant – the Bajagua project, to be built in Tijuana – has been batted around for years and, as of this writing, is still being debated.

On a less gloomy note, we noticed that the ominous hand-painted signs along Monument Road are now gone, and a Border Patrol guard informed us that illegal border crossings had been declining. He also cogently observed, "We don't have any room to talk about Mexico when you look at the way we treat our own beaches and oceans."

Even so, the latest issue for the beleaguered area is that the federal government has proposed building a "security barrier" that would encroach 150 feet into Border Field State Park. As one local environmental group put it, "The magnitude of the cut and fill proposed for the fence is totally unacceptable. We are concerned that the alteration of natural landscapes, slope stability, and sediment production will create untenable problems in the Border Highlands, the Tijuana River Valley and its estuary."

stopped, took some photographs, and turned back. Still, even in what some might term a hellhole, we admired the hard blue sky and small, puffy white clouds rimmed with silver linings, and the extensive marsh grasses of the estuary—among the last significant coastal wetlands in California.

While readying this edition, we discovered that the state has simply closed the park completely on weekdays, except for those entering either on foot or on horses. So Border Field is open for "normal" use only on weekends and some holidays. So what can you do here? Well, one time we saw a group of men disassembling a car.

The area is not without historic and environmental interest, however. The border with Mexico, which runs east from Border Field for

1,952 miles, was established on October 10, 1849. That was the date on which California was officially whisked away from Mexico to become a part of the United States. A cement monument makes note of this event, and informative placards recount both nations' histories and prehistories. Other signs contain tidbits about the ancient geological uplift that created this ruggedly beautiful beach and the wildlife that presumably still roams it.

Unfortunately, the words on most of the markers have been worn away by sun, sand, and surf. The spray-painted Spanish graffiti on the walls is more legible. More overwhelming than anything nature might devise is the sprawl of Tijuana, which comes right up to the fence. Tijuana is a city twice the size of San Diego that continues to grow at an alarming rate. It is the land of last hope for rural Mexicans who come looking for work or wait until dark to make the illegal stroll north. A sobering statistic: 400 people a year die while trying to cross illegally from Mexico to the United States. (Listen to the Bruce Springsteen song "Matamoras Banks" for a chilling account of one such casualty.) That number is greater than were ever killed trying to scale the Berlin Wall. And now the United States is constructing a veritable Berlin Wall along the border with Mexico with much the same purpose: to make sure that those on one side cannot enter the other.

One of the few pleasant pastimes that can be enjoyed at Border Field is riding horses. They can be rented in the area and ridden on designated trails in the adjoining Tijuana River National Estuarine Reserve.

For more information, contact Border Field State Park, 619/575-3613, www.parks.ca.gov.

BEACHES

A visit to Border Field offers up stark dichotomies: the lulling sound of crashing waves suddenly interrupted by the screech of an Immigration Service paddy wagon lurching from behind a clump of dried grass to snag another undocumented alien. Another contrast: a gorgeous stretch of wild, windswept sand surrounded by wildflowers, marshlands, and jagged geological formations—dotted with signs warning that swimming is prohibited due to raw sewage spills washing northward from Tijuana. Even when the water is sewage-free, the rip currents and in-shore holes can be nasty, and there's no lifeguard on duty. As a sign at the park entrance starkly puts it, Swimming and Wading Unsafe. Yes, Border Field State Park is a real party pooper.

◼ BORDER FIELD STATE PARK

Location: From I-5 near the Mexican border, take Dairy Mart Road exit and turn right. Follow Dairy Mart Road for 1.5 miles, then turn right on Monument Road and follow into park.
Parking/Fees: $5 entrance fee per vehicle on weekends; free for pedestrians and equestrians at all times
Hours: 9:30 A.M.–5 P.M. Pedestrians and equestrians are allowed on weekdays. Vehicles are allowed into the park only on weekends. Flooding may sometimes close the park even on weekends.
Facilities: restrooms, picnic tables, and fire pits
Contact: Tijuana Estuary Visitor Center, 619/575-3613

Imperial Beach

Depending on your perspective, Southern California—as a way of life and a state of mind—begins or ends at Imperial Beach (population 27,000). It is the southernmost beach town in California. Here you'll find the state's southernmost strip malls, trailer parks, libraries, baseball fields, and skateboard ramps—not to mention the southernmost McDonald's and Taco Bells. (Speaking of Taco Bell, we should point out that no one's running *for* the border in these parts; they're running *from* it.) You'll also find a modest-sized community of mostly middle-class citizens trying hard to ignore the looming presence of Tijuana, so close by that on smog-free days the bullring is visible from the beach.

Folks here make a concerted effort to sell the town as a placid resort, billing it as the "South Coast Hideaway." Still, the bottom line in Imperial Beach, as stated by a city booster in 2008, is this: "People don't stay here because we don't have the accoutrements that they want." On the positive side, Imperial Beach has a 2.5-mile beach, abundant year-round sunshine, and pleasant natural backdrops to the east (distant hills and mesas) and south (Tijuana Slough National Wildlife Refuge). Yes, Imperial Beach has a lot going for it. So why the hangdog expressions? Well, this is the beach town that has been most impacted by the sins of Tijuana. The issue of raw sewage and ocean contamination has been a hot one for decades. So has beach erosion, necessitating periodic sand-renourishment projects (though federal money for these Band-Aid solutions tends to dry up when the economy is stressed).

Two main drags, Palm and Coronado Avenues, lead through town to the ocean. These parallel routes are Imperial Beach's commercial corridors, lined with a random hodgepodge of liquor stores, taco huts, decrepit bars, pool halls, and countless car-related enterprises: dealers, repair shops, tire stores, and places to wash your ride. Imperial Beach has been endeavoring to replace its blighted neighborhoods (read: trailer parks) with new condos and apartment buildings. In its futile attempts at gentrification, Imperial Beach recalls Ashbury Beach, New Jersey. In both places, the more things change, the more they stay the same. Meantime, the latest twist is that Imperial Beach has turned to ecotourism to spur interest. Indeed, the **Tijuana River National Estuarine Research Reserve** (301 Caspian Way, 619/575-3613, visitors center 10 A.M.–5 P.M. Wed.–Sun.) is that rarity in California: a coastal wetland that hasn't been destroyed. Trail-riding can be done daily from a half-hour before sunrise to a half-hour after sunset.

Imperial Beach

© PARKE PUTERBAUGH

For more information, contact the Imperial Beach Chamber of Commerce, 702 Seacoast Drive, Imperial Beach, CA 91932, 619/424-3151, www.ib-chamber.biz.

BEACHES

Imperial Beach runs for 2.5 miles. This municipal beach's assets include the sturdy 1,500-foot Imperial Beach Pier, healthy surf and an army of healthy surfers, and the town's renovated Pier Plaza. This pier-side park complex includes picnic pavilions, shops, a play area, and a sculptural tribute to the sport of wave-riding called *Surfhenge*. (It looks like multicolored McDonald's arches.) Cleverly, Pier Plaza even provides surfboard-shaped benches to sit on. Posted snippets detail Imperial Beach's early history as a wave-rider's mecca. Every summer Imperial Beach celebrates Sandcastle Days, which culminates with the **U.S. Open Sandcastle Competition.** Held the last weekend in July, it is the world's longest-running sand-sculpting contest.

The surf at Imperial Beach is among the most challenging in San Diego County. In

TOUGH TIMES ON THE TIJUANA RIVER ESTUARY

As you watch any of the 340 bird species that have been spotted in the Tijuana River Valley, you'd never know that a raging controversy runs through the beautiful estuary. The Tijuana River Estuary is an integral part of California's remaining coastal wetlands, 90 percent of which have been lost to dredging, development, and pollution. Located between Border Field State Park and Imperial Beach, they are among the last wetlands in San Diego County.

Most of the Tijuana River runs through Mexico, draining 1,700 square miles. The five-mile tail end of the river cuts across the U.S. border and snakes through San Diego County, where it meets the ocean. Those five miles and the 3,000 acres of federal and private land drained by it have been battled over as intensely as any five miles of the western front in World War I. They are owned by private parties, the city of San Diego, the county of San Diego, the state of California, and the federal government, which administers the majority of it (2,531 acres). Each has an idea about how best to save the estuary from the many slings and arrows constantly hurled at it.

The best way to see the estuary is on foot. A free walker's guide to the Tijuana River Estuary is available from the Southwest Wetlands Interpretive Association (P.O. Box 575, Imperial Beach, CA 92032, 619/575-0550). This useful tool reveals the lay of the land – from footpaths and horse trails to hitching posts and overlooks. We recommend a look-see at this wonderful, threatened spot to anyone concerned about coastal ecology.

The **Tijuana River National Estuarine Research Reserve** – which also encompasses the Tijuana Slough National Wildlife Refuge – has a visitors center (301 Caspian Way, Imperial Beach, 619/575-3613). From here, one can access the estuary's trails. The visitors center is open Wednesday to Sunday, 10 A.M.-6 P.M. in summer, and to 5 P.M. in winter.

There is no better learning lab than the Tijuana River Estuary, where you can discover the difference between mudflats, tidal sloughs, uplands, riverbeds, and low, middle, and high marshes. Then there are the hundreds of species of plants and animals that live here. One of the tips in the walker's guide should be mandatory etiquette at every beach in the world: "Feel free to pick up as much litter as you like!"

fact, it was the first real big-wave surfing spot on the Southern California surfing scene, dating back to the 1940s. (Before Imperial Beach's incorporation in 1956, surfers called this sacred area "Tijuana Sloughs.") Today, surfers of all ages vie for space near the pier, which provides an excellent vantage point from which spectators can view their prodigious skills. After watching one particularly nice run by a blond surfer—during which he executed several 360-degree spin moves to keep abreast of his chosen wave—the grandfatherly chap next to us shouted down to him, "Good show!" The surfer shrugged and said, "No, I blew it!"

But he was obviously pleased that someone had noticed.

The downside is the danger that these powerful waves pose to the uninitiated. Each year the vigilant lifeguard squad in Imperial Beach makes upward of 600 rescues. In addition to strong surf, rip currents—some extending outward for three-quarters of a mile—are capable of pulling even the strongest swimmer under. (Be sure to check the daily advisories posted at the lifeguard stands.) This air of danger only adds to the edgy appeal of Imperial Beach for surfers and lifeguards alike. Incidentally, there are fewer restrictions on where you can surf in

Imperial Beach than on the more urbanized beaches elsewhere in Southern California. As one lifeguard said, "We are one of the last truly open beaches. You can surf anywhere."

Massive infusions of sand dredged from San Diego Bay have restored the Imperial Beach's width on several occasions, but it always seems to vanish during winter storms. On a recent visit, at the residential south end of Seacoast Drive, the beach was essentially nonexistent, the raging Pacific held back by riprap and prayers.

The newest sand-renourishment project, proposed in 2007, has aroused the ire of local surfers, who have complained that it might wreck the surfing at the legendary Tijuana Sloughs. They also worry about the quality of sand used, which would have practical and aesthetic impacts as well. The surfers have reason to worry. Dredge spoil dumped on local beaches in 2002 and 2005 turned the water murky and surfboards black. The fact that more sand is already needed testifies to the pointlessness and squandered expense of sand renourishment. And how's this for a no-win scenario? Their choice of sand is either a north county source, filled with cobblestones, or from the mouth of the Tijuana River, which is entrained with toxic pollutants.

This latest boondoggle is called the Silver Strand Shoreline Renourishment Project, and it's projected to last for 50 years, with sand infusions every decade. It is the largest such project on tap along the entire West Coast. Once again, the work is being done by the U.S. Army Corps of Engineers, the organization that's made a habit of fighting Mother Nature and losing. Actually, we the taxpayers wind up being the real losers, since we're footing the bill for their follies. The surfers are trying to introduce some sense into the debate by involving themselves as interested and informed parties. Without question they're capable of making better decisions than the hapless Corps. At present, the Corps is still looking for $60 million to fund their latest sandy crap shoot.

2 IMPERIAL BEACH

Location: Seacoast Drive between Palm and Encanto Avenues in Imperial Beach
Parking/Fees: metered street and lot parking
Hours: 24 hours
Facilities: lifeguards, restrooms, and showers
Contact: Imperial Beach Lifeguard Service, 619/628-1419; surf report, 619/595-3954

ACCOMMODATIONS

The **Seacoast Inn** (800 Seacoast Drive, 619/424-5183, $$), centerpiece of Imperial Beach's oceanfront, is currently undergoing renovation. Located just north of the pier, the landmark promises to be a bit more of a beacon on Imperial Beach's oceanfront. When completed, it will have 78 oceanview rooms and a renourished beach. But, take notice: Redevelopment had not even begun when this book went to press. In the meantime, you can bunk down at **Hawaiian Gardens Suite Hotel** (1031 Imperial Beach Blvd., 619/429-5303, $$).

COASTAL CUISINE

The most scenic dining spot in Imperial Beach is the **Tin Fish,** at the end of the Imperial Beach Pier (910 Seacoast Drive, 619/628-4214, $). Fried platters are the favorite, but you can opt for something healthier like grilled halibut or grilled calamari. And you can take in all the surfing and angling going on all around you. A good bet for seafood and breakfast is **IB Seafood and Breakfast** (809 Seacoast Drive, 619/429-1129, $$). Ask about fresh-fish specials at dinnertime. As for breakfast, what else but an IB High Surf Omelet (bacon, sausage, cheese, and onion)? Not that you'll have the stomach to surf after downing that leviathan. Also near the ocean is the **Beach Club Grille** (710 Seacoast Drive, 619/628-0777, $). Adjacent to Dunes Park playground, it's a good place to hit for deli fare or a gyro.

You won't have to wander far in this border town to find tolerable taco huts. Here are three of them: **Mi Ranchito Taco Shop** (805 Seacoast Drive, 619/424-8260, $), **Tacos Corita** (757 Seacoast Drive, 619/429-6565, $), and **El Tapatio's** (260 Palm Avenue, 619/423-3443, $). Over the years we've scarfed Mexican grub at all three establishments, leaving happily with full stomachs and the knowledge that we ate well for next to nothing.

NIGHTLIFE

Beer joints and pool halls line Palm and Coronado Avenues. **Ye Olde Plank Inn** (24 Palm Avenue, 619/423-5976) is the most popular of this lot. That is not exactly a ringing endorsement, as most of the guys we saw sported biker garb. One visitor here described the Plank as a cesspool of the dregs of the military and transplanted Midwesterners. (We'll bet he didn't say that to their faces.) The most appealing beachfront tavern is the **IB Forum** (1079 Seacoast Drive, 619/429-7507), which accurately bills itself as "the most southwesterly bar and grill in the U.S." You can grill your own steaks here.

San Diego

A thousand years ago, the land on which San Diego now stands was a paradise inhabited by the Kumeyaay. They thrived along the bountiful waters of this big bay, one of the largest natural harbors in the world. With Point Loma to the west, fish- and wildlife-rich marshlands to the south, and protective mountains to the east, they no doubt thanked the gods profusely for their good fortune.

Of course, fortunes like this don't remain secret for long. In the 16th century, Portuguese explorer Juan Rodríguez Cabrillo stumbled upon the Kumeyaays' bay. The last of the conquistadors, Cabrillo came in search of gold. Instead he sailed into this perfect harbor on September 28, 1542. He named it San Miguel and claimed it for his royal patrons. Then he sailed away. This one quick visit earned Cabrillo the distinction of having "discovered" the

West Coast. Cabrillo brought his knowledge of the Kumeyaays' paradise back to Europe with him. Sixty years later, explorer Sebastian Vizcaino sailed into San Miguel and renamed it San Diego de Alcalá.

On July 2, 1769, the Catholic mystic-priest Father Junípero Serra established the first Spanish mission in California on Presidio Hill in San Diego de Alcalá. More a charismatic visionary than a humble padre, Serra inaugurated an ambitious plan for his town, combining a military battalion with a Catholic parish into a philosophy of conquest that would become known as the "mission system." His mission was clear enough (to convert the heathen natives), and his system eventually spanned 21 settlements, a network that subjugated the native populations of California.

Serra's recruitment method was known as "the cross or the sword." By the time the Spanish overlords were finished, the Kumeyaay had been left either dead by the sword or dependent on the mercy of the cross. Old Town San Diego stands in testament to his legacy. Today it's mostly a shopping mall set among period buildings. Yet Old Town is home to Serra's original mission and chapel, where mass is still held every Sunday.

California remained loyal to Spain and then Mexico, after the latter won its independence in 1821. California was admitted to the United States and San Diego was incorporated in September 1850. San Diego County became the first county in California. In 1867, a fast-talking Easterner named Alonzo Horton purchased San Diego's entire waterfront and laid out a grid of streets upon which the business district was built. Even today, Horton's "new town" looks new, dominated by nondescript skyscrapers. A plaza stands in tribute to Horton—another upscale shopping and hotel area.

In 1884, the transcontinental railroad reached San Diego. In 1917, the U.S. Navy landed here, building shipyards and installations on every available scrap of land and creating a gray military presence that dominated San Diego until recent times. Because of the harbor, San Diego soon became the permanent base for the nation's largest West Coast fleet, numbering well over 100,000 personnel. This, of course, attracted military contractors, which subsisted on the government tab for years. However, the military downsizing of the early '90s hit San Diego particularly hard. The city rebounded with the nation's tech-driven economic upturn during the Clinton years. And while the war on terrorism may keep San Diego's naval installations and defense contractors occupied, the steady economic downturn of the Bush years, combined with problems peculiar to California, has had a sobering effect on San Diego's fortunes and self-image in the new millennium.

In some ways, San Diego is still a navy town, but it's been looking elsewhere for its identity. As the 17th-largest metropolitan area in the country, with a bayfront that is the envy of the world, it certainly has ample resources to draw upon. In fact, the area has swelled like a dry sponge dropped in a tidepool. Many people are retiring here, while others sail in as part of the leisure-boat crowd. The San Diego metro area's population is inching up on 3 million. That figure, it should be noted, includes not just the city of San Diego proper but surrounding communities that fall under its municipal umbrella, including Ocean Beach, Mission Beach, Pacific Beach, and La Jolla. Annually, the city receives 30,000 new residents and boasts about 15 million overnight visitors.

There is a reason for this prodigious immigration. The weather in San Diego is ideal for anyone who doesn't crave variety. Temperatures year-round rarely stray from the 70s. It seldom rains in the summer, and when it does, according to a local resident, people stare at the heavens as if witnessing a solar eclipse. Within easy reach are beautiful mountains and unique desert communities (including one with the intriguing name of Plaster City). There are zoos, museums, theme parks, and theaters galore. And, of course, there are 70 miles of ocean beaches in the county.

Over the years, self-promoting San Diego has adopted all of the following nicknames: Sports Town USA, Golf Land USA, America's Finest City, California's Oldest City, The Place Where California Began, California's Plymouth Rock. Even areas of dubious history or merit are trumped up into Disney-esque attractions, carrying touristy names such as Seaport Village and Gaslamp Quarter. Then there are genuinely worthwhile attractions such as Balboa Park, SeaWorld, and roughly 90 museums. Of course, negotiating spread-out San Diego requires a maze of superhighways. Interstates intertwine across the scorched brown terrain like seaweed, giving a novice driver headaches, twinges of anxiety, and watery eyes. You may hear otherwise, but there is smog in San Diego.

The pace of life here is deceptive. Though leisurely on the surface, the city throbs with an undercurrent of manic activity. Cars are in constant motion, glittering like metallic bugs in the dry heat as they scurry along the freeways. Bicycles, in-line skates, skateboards, Segways, unicycles, and even pogo sticks hound the heels of sedate pedestrians. Joggers saunter along the harborfront. Sailboats and yachts cut through the bay like stilettos. The race is on all the time, even if you can't figure out where the finish line is or what you get if you win. Perhaps an eternal round of golf.

There's been some real trouble in paradise of late. The city manager and city auditor were forced to quit in 2004 over a pension-fund scandal. The city's sitting mayor was a casualty of the brouhaha as well. He was replaced by an acting mayor who himself was quickly found guilty of taking bribes from a strip-club owner and imprisoned. Beyond the taint of political scandal, San Diego has suffered severely from the collapse of California's overheated real estate market in this decade. No surprise here: The median price of a home in San Diego has been running three times the national average. Foreclosures are soaring in a market hit especially hard by the sub-prime mortgage lending crisis. It didn't take a crystal ball to anticipate this as the inevitable outcome of bad planning by those in real estate, construction, investment banking, and mortgage lending, where greed routinely trumps common sense.

Even in tough times, the lure of San Diego is obvious. It starts at the water, with its vast and appealing harbor. Because our yacht was repossessed in a previous lifetime, we generally spend less time on the bay—except for a meal, a stroll along the Embarcadero's Marina Park, and a visit to Balboa Park—and head straight to the beaches of San Diego. That is where we encourage our readers to start and finish their experiences of this remarkable city. Each of the beach communities within reach of downtown San Diego—Coronado, Point Loma, Ocean Beach, Mission Beach, Pacific Beach—is covered in the following pages. Each has its own unique flavor and appeal.

For more information, contact the San Diego Convention and Visitors Bureau, 2215 India Street, San Diego, CA 92101, 619/236-1212, www.sandiego.org; Greater San Diego Chamber of Commerce, 402 West Broadway, San Diego, CA 92101, 619/544-1300, www.sdchamber.org; San Diego Visitor Information Center, 2688 East Mission Bay Drive, San Diego, CA 92109, 619/276-8200 or 800/422-4749, www.infosandiego.com.

RECREATION AND ATTRACTIONS

- **Bike/Skate Rentals:** Cheap Rentals, 3698 Mission Boulevard, Mission Beach, 858/488-9070; Hamel's, 708 Ventura Place, Mission Beach, 858/488-5050

- **Boat Cruise:** San Diego Harbor Excursion, 1050 North Harbor Drive, San Diego, 619/234-4111

- **Dive Shop:** Blue Escape Dive, 1617 Quivara Road #B, San Diego, 619/223-3483

- **Ecotourism:** H&M Landing, 2803 Emerson Street, San Diego, 619/224-1134 (whale-watching); Seal Tours, Seaport Village, 619/298-8687; La Jolla Kayak & Company, 2199 Avenida de la Playa, La Jolla, 619/459-1114

- **Fishing Charters:** Islandia Sportfishing, 1551 West Mission Bay Drive, San Diego, 619/222-1164

- **Marina:** Commercial Basin, Shelter Island, 619/291-3900; Sheraton, Harbor Island, San Diego, 619/291-2900

- **Piers:** Crystal Pier, Mission Boulevard at Garnet Avenue, Pacific Beach; Imperial Beach Pier, Seacoast Drive, Imperial Beach

- **Rainy Day Attraction:** Birch Aquarium, Scripps Institute, 2300 Expedition Way, La Jolla (I-5 at La Jolla Village Drive exit), 858/534-3474

- **Shopping/Browsing:** Gaslamp Quarter Downtown Historical District, Third and Fourth Avenues, San Diego

- **Surf Report:** 619/221-8884

- **Surf Shop:** South Coast Surf Shop, 5023 Newport Avenue, Ocean Beach, 619/223-7017; Bob's Mission Surf, 4320 Mission Boulevard, Mission Beach, 858/483-8837

- **Vacation Rentals:** Penny Realty, 4444 Mission Boulevard, San Diego, 858/272-3900 or 800/748-6704

Coronado

Coronado gleams with a gilded, moneyed loveliness that stands in stark contrast to the border-town blues of nearby Imperial Beach. Driving north from Imperial Beach along Silver Strand Boulevard, you pass from a land of no money to a land of new money. First you notice the yachts that fill the Glorietta Bay Marina, their long masts standing as tall and straight as a fistful of pencils jammed in a cup. Then you realize that the price of gas has jumped by 10 percent in the space of 10 miles. Finally, turning onto Orange Avenue, which leads into downtown Coronado, you roll by a historic old resort hotel and rows of opulent private homes fronted by lawns that are better tended than country-club putting greens.

The rich have perched alongside the naval air base on this spit of land enfolding San

Diego Bay. They have erected high-rise condos, private estates, and tropical gardens where flowers of flaming crimson, deep purple, and passion pink add a splash of color to what would be, in its natural state, an arid landscape. Coronado (population 22,850) is a verdant garden by the sea, an oasis made possible by sprinkler systems, cheap immigrant labor, and big money.

The story of Coronado's founding is emblematic of how it went in the glory days of California's birth: Some wealthy guy would get an idea, and all of a sudden a desert would magically become a Technicolor resort in year-round bloom. Coronado's past is linked with some of the wealthiest figures in California's history, and their presence sets a standard of luxurious living that endures to this day. The founding fathers of Coronado are railroad tycoon Elisha Babcock Jr. and piano magnate H. L. Story. The two spent time hunting on the wild, majestic Coronado peninsula, enjoying the place so much that they eventually switched their quarry from rabbits and quail to tourist dollars. The pair formed a syndicate, the Coronado Beach Company, and bought the entire peninsula for $110,000 in 1885.

Ground was broken on the Hotel del Coronado in January 1887. It was envisioned as a wondrous resort that would become the "talk of the Western world." Barely a year later, "the Del," as it is informally known, was open for business. Babcock and Story were later joined in their venture by John D. Spreckels, a wealthy San Francisco–reared heir to a sugar fortune who sailed his yacht down to San Diego in 1887, dropped anchor, and essentially brought the city to life. He built the first wharves in San Diego's natural harbor and linked the city to the outside world with the construction of the San Diego, Arizona, and Eastern Railway. He also bought newspapers, installed streetcars, and founded a bank. To his credit, he ensured that the development of San Diego proceeded along pleasingly aesthetic lines, seeing to it that the city was generously laid out with parks and that the parks were planted with his favorite flowers: geraniums. His financial stake in the Del grew to the point that he bought out the other partners by the turn of the century. There have been only four owners since Spreckels, and in the new millennium the Hotel del Coronado projects a casual splendor, much as it did a century ago.

If you can afford it, Coronado is the ideal vacation town, as tourism is the only industry in what is otherwise an upscale bedroom and retirement community. There's evidence of money everywhere. Even the sand on Coronado's beaches is speckled with what looks like gold dust, glittering every time it's washed over by a wandering wave. The feel-good feeling radiates outward from the Hotel del Coronado to the downtown area, where a graceful S curve carries motorists through a squeaky-clean shopping district of modestly upscale shops and restaurants along Orange Avenue. Coronado's cafés and stores service the needs of locals and tourists alike. Everyone casually strolls, bikes, or in-line skates along the sun-dappled streets in search of swimwear, surfboards, frozen yogurt, and real estate.

Continue away from the beach along Fourth Avenue and soon you'll be headed out of town via the narrow San Diego–Coronado Bridge, a breathtaking engineering marvel that arches like a roller coaster and makes a 90-degree turn at mid-span. It's high enough that navy destroyers can pass beneath it. It also attracts would-be jumpers, judging from signs lining the bridge that offer a phone number for suicide counseling. Incidentally, in 2002 they stopped charging a toll to cross the San Diego–Coronado Bridge.

The naval presence is everywhere. The Naval Air Station North Island claims to be the birthplace of naval aviation, based on the fact that a navy lieutenant transferred here to receive flight instruction in 1910. More history was made in 1927, when Charles Lindbergh took off from here for New York and then embarked upon his famous first transatlantic flight. The Naval Air Station North Island is the hub of Naval Base Coronado (NBC). These seven affiliated naval installations collectively occupy 57,000 acres and employ 36,000 personnel. It is the largest command in the Southwest United States. In addition to the Naval Air Station, whose constantly incoming and outgoing flights might keep you awake, amphibious units are trained at Naval Amphibious Base (NAB) Coronado, located along Silver Strand between San Diego Bay and the ocean. Interestingly, a six-building complex at NAB Coronado was inadvertently constructed in the shape of a swastika. Oops.

For more information, contact the Coronado Visitors Bureau, 1100 Orange Avenue, Coronado, CA 92118-3418, 619/437-8788 or 800/622-8300, www.coronado.ca.us; or the Coronado Chamber of Commerce, 875 Orange Avenue, Suite 102, Coronado, CA 92118, 619/435-9260, www.coronadochamber.com.

BEACHES

Heading north from Imperial Beach along Silver Strand Boulevard, you begin to see the pipe rooftops of Coronado Cays, clustered together so tightly that the development looks like one continuous orange roof. Along the south side of the bay is the South Bay Marine Biological Study Area, a wildlife refuge that affords visitors a close look at a wetland environment. A nature trail leads into the study area, where bird-watching is excellent. On the ocean side of the highway, **Silver Strand State Beach,** a long beach occupying a skinny splinter of land no more than two football fields wide, connects Imperial Beach with Coronado. In season, RVs are jammed together as close as possible while still allowing their occupants to open the doors. The 2.5-mile beach can take on all comers, with parking for more than 1,000 vehicles. Being so far south, the waters here are as swimmable as any in California from the standpoint of temperature, topping off at around 70 degrees by late summer.

Coronado Shores Beach fills the breach between Silver Strand State Beach and Coronado City Beach. It's accessible via the Coronado Shores condo development—a ghastly, humongous array of seaside towers—and is widely used by surfers, swimmers, shell collectors, and anglers.

Coronado City Beach (a.k.a. Central Beach) runs for 1.5 miles, from the Hotel del Coronado up to the airstrip at the Naval Air Station North Island. The beach is wide and flat, dimpled with half-formed dunes. The north end of the beach is locally known as Dog Beach, for obvious reasons. There's even some tidepooling to be done. To our inquiring eyes on a recent visit, the early-summer waves were tame, and the beachgoers were similarly benign.

A wall of boulders stands where the beach meets Ocean Boulevard, which has plentiful on-street parking. In Coronado, parking doesn't seem to be as horrific a problem as it does elsewhere in Southern California beach towns. On a gorgeous Saturday over a Fourth of July weekend, we found metered, on-street parking both available and reasonably priced at a quarter an hour—a good omen. Away from the beachfront, between Sixth and Ninth Streets along Orange Avenue, free street parking borders a lovely green park.

Beaches, in fact, abound on both the bay and the ocean—28 miles of them in all. Along the bayfront is the city-owned Glorietta Bay Beach, which is a park with a small calm-water beach. Renting a bike is a good way to check them out; 15 miles of bike paths wind their way around Coronado and down toward Silver Strand State Beach. Bikes and 'blades can be rented at **Bikes and Beyond** (1201 First Avenue, 619/435-7180) and **Little Sam's Island and Beach Fun** (1343 Orange Avenue, 619/435-4068).

❸ SILVER STRAND STATE BEACH

Location: 4.5 miles south of Coronado, at 5000 Silver Strand Boulevard/Highway 75
Parking/Fees: $8 entrance fee per vehicle;

camping fees $25–30 per night beachfront, $20–25 per night inland, plus $7.50 reservation fee

Hours: summer 8 A.M.–8 P.M.; winter 8 A.M.–7 P.M.

Facilities: lifeguards, restrooms, showers, picnic area, and fire pits

Contact: Silver Strand State Beach, 619/435-5184

4 CORONADO SHORES BEACH

Location: at the south end of Coronado, at the Coronado Shores condo complex, on Silver Strand Boulevard/Highway 75

Parking/Fees: free parking lot

Hours: 6 A.M.–11 P.M.

Facilities: none

Contact: Coronado Recreation Services, 619/522-7342

5 CORONADO CITY BEACH

Location: in Coronado at Ocean Boulevard and F Avenue

Parking/Fees: metered street parking

Hours: 6 A.M.–11 P.M.

Facilities: lifeguards, restrooms, picnic area, and fire rings

Contact: Coronado Recreation Services, 619/522-7342

ACCOMMODATIONS

On the outdoor deck of the **Hotel del Coronado** (1500 Orange Avenue, 619/435-6611, www.hoteldel.com, $$$$), we heard a quintet playing a mix of blues and jazz. An elderly black man was singing, "I got the blues." He must have been the only one within earshot who did, as the crowd—a well-heeled lot who were either reclining on chaise lounges amid a sea of red-and-white umbrellas, playing tennis, or swimming in

the Olympic pool—were having the time of their lives. A food kiosk offered "super burgers," "yummy hot dogs," and "healthy chicken breasts." It was quite a sight: a herd of happy people renting a small piece of paradise, basking in the midday sun. On another deck Frank Sinatra could be heard belting out the words "I'm king of the hill, top of the heap, A number-one!" His lyrics were reaching the right audience, bathing the upscale resort crowd in positive reinforcement.

The centerpiece of Coronado, the Del is a vast, capacious resort that's far more inviting than your typically stuffy corporate high-rise hotel. The grounds are impeccably well maintained, with walkways that meander among tropical greenery and such exotica as the rare "dragon tree" (imported from China in the 1920s). The Del lives up to its reputation by sweating the details so that pampered guests can take their ease. Most of them seem to realize that lying out on a breezy deck in a chaise lounge, with an icy drink and a gaggle of musicians tooting jazz on a small bandstand, is what a vacation is all about.

The Del claims to be the largest full-service beachfront resort on the Pacific Coast. We've certainly seen nothing in our travels to dispute that. The resort encompasses 689 rooms, and every one is different. Built in 11 months according to plans that were improvised day by day, the hotel is one of the architectural wonders of the Western world. At the time of its construction, it was the largest electrically lighted structure outside New York City. Four hundred rooms are originals, dating from 1888; the rest are in a wing constructed in the 1960s. Try to stay in the main part of the hotel. This four-story marvel rambles around in a rectangle that surrounds a green courtyard filled with palm trees and brightly colored flowers. The on-premises amenities include two giant outdoor pools, six tennis courts, volleyball nets, and a croquet green. Just be advised that you will pay dearly for all this privileged access, as oceanfront rooms start at around $480 per night. However, they were offering a "third night free" as a recent promotion, so perhaps business isn't booming.

More impressive than the statistics is the feeling of informal elegance that fills the place. Rambling around the Del is like exploring a rich old relative's mansion. If you come here, you may be living above your station (as we most definitely were), but you'll be made to feel right at home. "You've stayed with us before?" asks a bellhop as you arrive, as if assuming you've returned to renew an old friendship. The hotel's brick-red turrets and gleaming white Victorian exterior make it look less like a hotel than a castle. Indeed, it is a national landmark that has played host to 11 U.S. presidents. Hollywood seems to like the place, too. *Some Like It Hot,* starring Marilyn Monroe, was filmed here, and the Emerald City in *The Wizard of Oz* was patterned after the Hotel del Coronado's castle-like design.

Across the street is the mission-style **El Cordova** (1351 Orange Avenue, 619/435-4131, www.elcordovahotel.com, $$$), whose 40 rooms are like small apartments, tucked into stairwells around a brick courtyard of ground-level shops and restaurants. Originally a private mansion built in 1902, when the area was still relatively rural, El Cordova opened as a hotel in 1930 and is currently maintained as one of the most homey and nicely appointed suite-style hotels we've encountered in our coastal travels.

Over on the bay, the former mansion of sugar baron John D. Spreckels is the centerpiece of the **Glorietta Bay Inn** (1630 Glorietta Boulevard, 619/435-3101, $$$), a relaxed but regal inn. Many rooms overlook the bay, while others face out on gardens. The setting is quiet, yet downtown Coronado is just a few walkable blocks away. And rooms start at $185, which offers some relief from the other venues hereabouts. The staff is unusually friendly and attentive. We're forever in their debt for finding and forwarding a pricey computer accessory we left behind on one visit.

COASTAL CUISINE

The best and most neighborly place to start the day is **Coronado Bakery** (1206 Ocean Avenue, 619/435-9272, $), which is a locals' favorite, and one of ours, too. You've got to try the "glazed rings" (doughnuts) or muffins (e.g., pumpkin raisin walnut bran) and watch the world jog by as you ingest delicious calories from a streetside table.

We had our first encounter with healthy, low-fat Mexican cuisine (no, that's not necessarily an oxymoron) in Coronado, courtesy of a fast-food chain called **La Salsa!** (1360 Orange Avenue, 619/435-7778, $). The legend printed on the beverage cups relates the chain's culinary philosophy: "No can openers. No microwaves. No freezers. No lard. Skinless chicken. Lean steak." We ordered vegetable tacos and watched the cook carefully slice onions and tomatoes, grill and place them on a soft taco, slather on black beans, and top it all off with shredded cheese, lettuce, avocado wedges, and fresh cilantro. Customers can ladle on salsa from a salsa bar, choosing from four grades of heat. Although the California Burrito has 18 grams of fat (it's the avocado's fault), by Mexican food standards even this is lean cuisine. La Salsa! has franchises all over Southern California, including locations in La Jolla, Pacific Beach, and Newport Beach. Coastal travelers craving a Mexican meal that won't send them down the road to a coronary bypass should keep this name handy.

Good-quality Mexican food in a sit-down environment is served at **Miguel's Cocina** (1351 Orange Avenue, 619/437-5237, $$), in the courtyard of El Cordova. It's known for fish tacos, which we can unhesitatingly recommend. Also very good are calamari (sauteed squid steak) and chicken (charbroiled free-range chicken) served on a *torta* roll with avocado, tomato, lettuce, and sauces.

Another reasonably priced and down-to-earth Coronado eatery is the **Fish Company** (1007 C Avenue, 619/435-3945, $$), a fresh-fish market and outdoor café with catch-of-the-day specials and a sushi bar.

On the bayside is the locally popular **Bay Beach Cafe** (1201 First Street, 619/435-4900, $$). Set among a dockside bazaar called Ferry Landing Marketplace, it looks out on the San Diego skyline. It's especially good at dinner, when seafood specials turn up on the menu. Incidentally, the San Diego Bay Ferry shuttles commuters between San Diego's B Street Pier, Coronado's Ferry Landing Marketplace, and the Naval Air Station North Island.

At the upper end of the scale is the posh and expensive **Azzura Point** (4000 Coronado Bay Road, 619/424-4477, $$$$), at Loews Coronado Bay Resort. You'll pay $25–60 per person for its culinary innovation and world-class views. Though Azzura Point lost an executive chef to the newly opened Nine-Ten in La Jolla, it remains one of the choicest "big occasion" restaurants in the San Diego area. Try the salmon in black truffle sauce or 10-spice ahi tuna. **Chez Loma French Bistro** (1132 Loma Avenue, 619/435-0661, $$$) puts a French twist on fresh California ingredients in a romantic setting. It has the added advantage of history, occupying a landmark building dating from 1889.

Over at the Hotel del Coronado, the **Crown-Coronet Room** (1500 Orange Avenue, 619/435-6611, $$$$) has served kings, presidents, movie stars, sheiks, and tycoons from all over the world. It is the largest of six restaurants on the premises. The room is as long as a football field, and the ceiling is 33 feet high, making it one of the largest freestanding wood structures in North America. At ground level, the menu tends toward "progressive continental" preparations, and the panoramic view is as delectable as the food. The most formal dining room at the Del is the **Prince of Wales Room** (1500 Orange Avenue, 619/435-6611, $$$$). We were advised of the dress code by our bellhop: "California formal—which means coat and tie and shoes."

Finally, a popular afternoon or after-dinner stop is **MooTime Creamery** (1025 Orange Avenue, 619/435-2422, $), a retro dessert diner with a life-size Elvis Presley sculpture out front. It also has a smaller unit inside the Hotel del Coronado.

NIGHTLIFE

Don't come to Coronado expecting nightlife. In fact, you can expect to be largely free of it. (Sometimes this is a blessing.) Your choices on the Coronado side of the San Diego–Coronado Bridge are pretty much limited to a handful of Irish pubs along Orange Avenue. The busiest of these is **McP's Irish Pub & Grill** (1107 Orange Avenue, 619/435-5280), which has been around since 1982 (it was founded by a former Navy SEAL) and bills itself as "Coronado's hottest night spot." By the standards of low-key Coronado, McP's does get fairly raucous.

For some serious whoopee head over the bridge to San Diego, which deposits you on Harbor Drive. Then proceed north to Fifth Avenue, which leads into downtown San Diego and its bustling Gaslamp Quarter district. There you'll find an abundance of restaurants and nightclubs.

Point Loma

Heading out to Point Loma from Ocean Beach, the land rises—first gently, then steeply—until you're high above the beaches and the bay. From this promontory the ocean glitters like a diamond choker and the cliffs take on a deep red hue at dusk. The area of Point Loma that enjoys these views, roughly between Ocean Beach and the Naval Ocean System Center, looks to be one of the choicest places to live in San Diego.

For a free glimpse of some of the most dramatic scenery on the peninsula, drive along Sunset Cliffs Boulevard from Point Loma Avenue to Ladera Street. This area is known as Sunset Cliffs Park; rather than an actual picnic-and-Frisbee green space, it is a series of parking areas and dirt trails that run along cliffs, allowing you to scuttle down like a crab to the edge of a heart-stopping drop-off. Some determined surfers and divers make their way down the steep paths to the sandy and rocky coves below. Be cautious, however; cliffs here are succumbing to wave-driven erosion at an alarming rate. Several parking turnouts have been closed, and signs at other turnouts warn visitors to keep a safe distance.

To continue out Point Loma, turn off Sunset Cliffs Boulevard onto Hill Street—an aptly named vertical grade—and then hang a right onto Catalina Boulevard/Highway 209. This becomes Cabrillo Memorial Drive and leads out to Cabrillo National Monument at the tip of the peninsula. The landform narrows as you pass through the gates of the Naval Ocean System Center and past a large military cemetery filled with small white crosses. This is **Fort Rosecrans National Cemetery,** and it spreads along the rolling contours of the peninsula—as tranquil a resting place as Arlington National Cemetery.

At **Cabrillo National Monument,** a fee of $5 per car will give you access to a stone statue of the Spanish conquistador and explorer Juan Rodríguez Cabrillo; views over San Diego Bay and Coronado; and the **Old Point Loma Lighthouse,** a harbor light and coastal beacon that illuminated the coast from 1855 to 1891. A skylit visitors center houses exhibits on Cabrillo's voyage and a well-stocked bookstore and gift shop.

For hiking and nature study, there's a one-mile (one-way) trail on the bay side and tidepools on the ocean side. Also on the bay side, inside the crook formed where Point Loma bends south, are two islands created in the 1960s from dredge spoil. ("Dredge spoil" is the nasty stuff sucked off the bay or ocean floor to deepen a channel for boat traffic.) The resulting sandbanks were christened **Shelter Island** and **Harbor Island,** and developers poured millions into building high-rise resorts, restaurants, and yacht basins. Familiar hotel and motel chains (Sheraton, Best Western, Holiday Inn) have perched upon these artificial paradises. Both are slanted to boaters and convention crowds, though Shelter Island has the decided advantage of a sandy beach.

For more information, contact the San Diego Peninsula Chamber of Commerce, P.O. Box 6015, San Diego, CA 92166, www .peninsulachamber.com.

Ocean Beach

In the medical profession it's a maxim that a patient's condition either improves or worsens over time, which is another way of saying that nothing remains the same for very long. The same bit of wisdom holds true for beach towns. Having taken the pulse of the California coast at regular intervals over the past quarter century, we've discovered that it's possible to come back to a community after several years' absence and sense immediately whether it's gone up or down. Ocean Beach, happily, has gone up. During our earliest visits we found it to be a low-rent slum by the sea. In an earlier book, we bluntly described it as "a sub-Coney Island maze of dirty streets, litter-strewn parking lots, sun-faded storefronts, and rough-looking bars." That no longer is true. Ocean Beach—or "O.B." for short—has gotten a much-needed makeover. And while no one will mistake it for La Jolla just yet, it's a comfortably funky beach town with just enough upscale refurbishing to inspire visitors to stick around rather than hurry away. It's possibly the hippest community in San Diego.

That is to say, Ocean Beach (population 28,000) has improved in much-needed ways, but not to the point that it has become unrecognizable. The community is a mix of the raunchy, the respectable, and the alternative. On one side of a street you'll see a decrepit bungalow occupied by ragtag post-hippies drinking in the yard. On the other side will sit a well-tended house with a neatly clipped lawn and a new coat of paint. The two opposing sensibilities—upscale and downtrodden—are literally staring each other down, though apparently coexisting.

The heart of Ocean Beach is along Newport Avenue from Sunset Cliffs Boulevard till it ends at the beach. What used to be an ugly array of failing liquor stores and five-and-dimes now runs the gamut from decent, lively burger joints for the surfer crowd to trendy restaurants with neon-scripted names. Most of the merchants are local; franchises are frowned upon. The sidewalks are clean and litter-free. Where once was a liquor store is now a fitness center. Even the local tattoo parlor seems vaguely respectable, offering custom tattooing "in the San Diego tradition." Aqua-colored tiles have been glued in a line along the curb with the names of local businesses inscribed on them.

For more information, contact the San Diego Peninsula Chamber of Commerce, P.O. Box 6015, San Diego, CA 92166, www .peninsulachamber.com.

BEACHES

Ocean Beach has gone to the dogs. We mean that literally and, oddly enough, positively. Where Voltaire Street runs out at the beach is **Ocean Beach Park.** At the north end is Dog Beach, a stretch of sand given over to the frolics of our canine friends. The sign reads: "Welcome to Dog Beach. This is a dog 'free' beach. Leashes are not required." Dogs do indeed have the run of the place. Their owners stand off to the side like helpless chaperones at a party gone haywire. The canine revelers scamper and yap; dig holes as if tunneling to China; sniff one another, fore and aft; relieve themselves indiscriminately; and run in and out of the water with tails wagging. In other words, they generally behave no differently than humans at the beach. We saw no fights, no snarling territorial disputes—just a happy pack of mutts and purebreds alike set free by their owners to romp to their hearts content. We should all get along so well. A postscript on water quality, however: It's awful off Dog Beach, so leave the scampering in the surf to the dogs.

Just up from Ocean Beach Park is **Ocean Beach City Beach,** a mile-long strand of municipal beach with the pier as its heart and soul. The ocean itself is unquestionably dangerous, due to both rough surf and polluted water. According to the head of lifeguard operations for San Diego County, "My impression is that Imperial Beach and Ocean Beach and the south end of Black's Beach are the most treacherous in San Diego. They have the strongest rip currents that are consistently pulling."

Surfers congregate around the sturdy, T-shaped concrete pier. At 1,971 feet, it's the longest on the West Coast. Midway out is a café serving hot coffee and good, hearty food. We walked out on the pier and watched a group of surfers waiting for the right wave. To us, watching surfers in action is nearly as much fun as surfing itself. They bob up and down on the swells in their wet suits, making small talk until…look out, here comes a monster! Just before it starts to curl, they steer into it, emerging astride their boards in a shower of flying foam while negotiating the sloping face of the spilling wave with perfect body English. Before it breaks on the beach, the surfers U-turn out of it and resume a belly-down position on the board, paddling back out to wait on another ride.

For the adventurous, the south end of Ocean Beach, along treacherous Sunset Cliffs Boulevard, offers numerous breathtaking views of the rocky coastline. A dirt parking lot at the end of Cornish Drive and a stairwell at the end of Ladera Street lead to a small rocky beach. The area is known as **Sunset Cliffs Park.** Various esoteric and locally known surfing spots, bearing such colorful names as "North Garbage" and "Bird Shit," can be found along the length of Sunset Cliffs Boulevard between Point Loma Avenue and Ladera Street.

6 SUNSET CLIFFS PARK

Location: Sunset Cliffs Boulevard between Ladera Street and Point Loma Avenue in Ocean Beach

© PARKE PUTERBAUGH

Ocean Beach

Parking/Fees: free parking lot at Cornish Drive and Ladera Street
Hours: 24 hours
Facilities: restrooms
Contact: San Diego Coastline Parks, 619/221-8901; surf report, 619/221-8884

⁊ OCEAN BEACH CITY BEACH

Location: 1950 Abbott Street in Ocean Beach
Parking/Fees: metered public lots and street parking
Hours: 4 A.M.–2 A.M.
Facilities: restrooms and lifeguards
Contact: Ocean Beach Recreation Center, 619/531-1527; surf report, 619/221-8884

⁸ OCEAN BEACH PARK

Location: in Ocean Beach at the end of Voltaire Street
Parking/Fees: metered parking lot

Hours: 4 A.M.–2 A.M.
Facilities: lifeguards, restrooms, showers, and picnic area
Contact: San Diego Regional Parks, 619/235-1169; surf report, 619/221-8884

ACCOMMODATIONS

The choices are limited and, cool as Ocean Beach may be for a day trip, you probably are better off staying elsewhere in San Diego. Still, the **Ocean Beach Hotel** (5080 Newport Avenue, 619/223-7191, www.obhotel.com, $) is a surfer's dream: plain, utilitarian, and cheap. The **Ocean Villa Motel** (5142 West Point Loma Boulevard, 619/224-3481, $$) is a bit nicer and takes pains to enforce a "no pets/no parties" policy. Rooms start at $170.

COASTAL CUISINE

Set in a typical bungalow that is the architectural trademark of Ocean Beach, **The Bungalow** (4996 West Point Loma Boulevard, 619/224-2884, $$) offers French/Continental cuisine at moderate prices. The house specialty is duck, but fish and chicken dishes are good as well.

At the other end of the scale, **Hodads** (5010 Newport Avenue, 619/224-4623, $) claims to serve the world's best burgers, proudly hanging a McDonald's-dissing sign that reads: "Under 99 billion sold." Another sign conveys the hang-loose atmosphere of the place: "No shirt, no shoes, no problem." The burgers are great messy slabs of beef stuck between a big bun and served in a basket. One table was fashioned from the sawed-off front of a VW bus. A buzzing hive of surfers chomps away at all hours, making a racket while gnawing on burgers the size of boogie boards.

NIGHTLIFE

Across the street from Hodads, the **South Beach Bar and Grill** (5059 Newport Avenue, 619/226-4577) is a great place to eat and/or down a few. We downed a few, eyeing the action on the pier from barstools pulled up to the picture window. The brew of choice is Hale's Pale Ale (say that three times fast), poured frosty cold from the tap. The restaurant serves fresh grilled thresher shark tacos, Baja fish tacos, and ceviche cocktail, among a full menu of other tasty seafood appetizers and entrées. While we were there, Bob Marley was playing on the sound system, while the San Diego Padres were on the boob tube. At a stool adjacent to ours, a prototypical beach girl with sun-damaged hair and reddened face reverently remarked to her male consort, "The ocean—what an amazing thing." We toasted this truism with raised mugs as the last rays of the day glinted off the distant waves.

Two spots for live music in Ocean Beach are **Winston's Beach Club** (1921 Bacon Street, 619/222-6822) and **Dream Street** (2228 Bacon Street, 619/222-8131). You might hear rock, reggae, punk, or cover bands with names like Downpour and Fortress.

Mission Beach

Mission Beach and Pacific Beach—neighboring communities welded together by paved, three-mile Ocean Front Walk—complement one another. This stretch of San Diego's shoreline epitomizes what a trip to a Southern California beach ought to be. Mission Beach, with a population of around 6,000, is the smaller of the two fraternal beach towns. Each is a "Community of San Diego," which is to say, they're not technically autonomous, though in reality they seem quite disconnected from San Diego proper.

It is not until you've made your way to the Mission Beach/Pacific Beach strand that you actually feel as if you're entering the pumping aorta of a true California beach town. You know, the kind you've always heard about: skateboards, roller skates, and in-line skates, volleyball on the beach, surfboards, surf shops, surf bars, surf bums, surf bunnies, and more bronzed flesh than you'll see on any 10 MTV Spring Break specials. Mission Beach is a great, relaxed party town where college students from UC San Diego and other nearby schools live the beach life to its fullest, majoring in sun, surf, sand, suds, and good times, in addition to whatever it is they're purportedly studying up the hill in La Jolla. Our observation is that surfers and other twenty-somethings are happily non-materialistic, living in the outdoors beside the ocean with a few pairs of cutoff jeans and a diet of cheap tacos and beer. Who needs more?

Mission Beach, though limited in area as a peninsula, is wall-to-wall real estate. In that sense, it is indistinguishable from Pacific Beach. Added to the eclectic mix of types who come here—from families and preppies to punks and the homeless—is a veneer of understated civility and good, clean fun that wasn't always evident before. This renaissance was symbolically ushered in by the 1990 reopening of **Belmont Park,** an antique amusement park and shopping area with a mountainous red, white, and blue roller coaster (the 77-year-old, 73-foot-high Giant Dipper) that defines the revived spirits of the town. More moms, pops, and kids are coming to Mission Beach, yet it still retains a tolerant attitude toward fun in the sun. This is important, as no less an authority than Sir Kenneth Clark proclaimed tolerance to be the key element of all civilizations.

Perhaps the scene around here takes its relaxed cue from the beat cops. They wear shorts, ride bikes, mingle, laugh, and eat ice cream cones like everyone else. They don't needlessly provoke confrontations; in fact, they spend a good deal of time defusing them. Even the homeless have found a haven of sorts in Mission Bay Park, a nice swath of green across from Belmont Park where they loll on the grass next to their shopping carts. Tanned redder than rare roast beef, they chat, drink from bags, and pass out without fanfare. Again, tolerance is the key.

Two different waterfronts are available to visitors here: the ocean and the bay. They offer opposing but equally appealing beach styles. The oceanfront was, is, and always will be *Animal House* and *American Graffiti* rolled into one. Mission Beach is not unlike Mardi Gras, except that it goes on for months instead of days. The human parade provides endless hours of spectator sport available only in Southern California. Strolling Ocean Front Walk, the paved oceanfront promenade that runs along Mission and Pacific Beaches, on any summer day is like walking along fraternity row during Rush Week. Shirtless guys clutch tall beers and lean off balconies of their rented apartments, passing judgment on the human parade below or squirting one another with water guns, while bikini-clad beauties casually lean back in chaise lounges and toy with mixed drinks and sunscreen, lathering their lithe bodies while the guys leer and yelp and yahoo. We saw a pet pig on someone's patio, strutting and wagging its tail like a dog. Meanwhile, one sun-bronzed fellow calmly stood atop his skateboard while two leashed, panting dogs gamely pulled him down the boardwalk like miniature huskies.

The scene on Mission Bay is more middle-class than back-of-the-class. Executive types and their families play badminton on putting-green-type grass along the water. Barbecue grills are on display, as are American flags. Catamarans are lashed to the dock or pulled onto the sand. Another three-mile paved track, Bay Side Walk, runs along the water, but the pace back here is more leisurely, less chaotic. It is most popular with joggers, who no doubt appreciate the safety factor. The houses and villas are a pleasant and eclectic blend of architectural styles, and they're fun to study while strolling beside the bay.

Our advice to novice visitors is to leave the car at the motel and rent bikes at one of the outfitters on Ocean Front Walk. Mission Beach has devoted only a limited amount of its precious open space to parking. If you do drive in Mission Beach, try to park on the bay-front, at Mission Bay Aquatic Center. To get there from Mission Boulevard (the main drag), turn east toward the bay on Santa Clara Place and follow it into the lot. It is within walking distance of the beach as well as a host of great bars and restaurants.

For more information, contact the San Diego Visitor Information Center, 2688 East Mission Bay Drive, San Diego, CA 92109, 858/276-8200 or 800/422-4749, www.info sandiego.com.

BEACHES

South Mission Beach begins at the channel that leads into San Diego Bay. The beach is especially wide and suitable for volleyball here. In fact, this is a very recreation oriented beach, with basketball courts and permissible areas to play "Over the Line." The central axis in **Mission Beach** is at the foot of Ventura Street, by Belmont Park, the main lifeguard stand, and a cluster of shops and restaurants. Mission Beach has designated areas for board surfing, bodysurfing, and swimming. Water conditions are updated on a board outside the lifeguard station (e.g., "Lots of rip currents and deep holes on the inside of the surf zone. Ask us where to swim."). Mission Beach runs up to, and into, Pacific Beach. It's neither clear nor important where one ends and the other begins, as it is all one happy, boardwalked, two-mile strand, from Mission Bay Channel to Crystal Pier.

On Ocean Front Walk, a human comedy that would have amused the French writer Honoré de Balzac glides past on bikes, in-line skates, shopping carts, and anything else to which wheels can be affixed. Somehow they don't collide, even though all are traveling at different speeds. In the midst of all this sauntered an old crone with a Hefty sack full of returnable cans and bottles, riffling through the trash cans for more. A gang of sun- and booze-battered longhairs of late-1960s vintage came riding around the corner on low-to-the-ground banana bikes that looked like something our sisters played on when they were six. It is all in the spirit of Mission Beach, a town where the laugh track runs continuously.

One summer day, we waded along the ocean's edge for a good distance. The water, at first cold to our feet, felt good and warmed quickly. Mission Beach, incidentally, appears friendly to surfers of all skill levels. The surf is more forgiving to beginners than La Jolla's storied beaches, but under the right swell conditions, Mission Beach also presents challenges for experts.

9 SOUTH MISSION BEACH

Location: south end of Mission Boulevard, from Avalon Place down to Mission Bay Channel in Mission Beach
Parking/Fees: free parking lot
Hours: 4 A.M.-2 A.M.
Facilities: lifeguards, restrooms, and showers
Contact: San Diego Coastline Parks, 619/221-8901; San Diego Regional Parks, 619/531-1527; surf report, 619/221-8884

10 MISSION BEACH

Location: Ventura Place at Mission Boulevard in Mission Beach

Parking/Fees: free parking lots
Hours: 4 A.M.-2 A.M.
Facilities: lifeguards and restrooms
Contact: San Diego Coastline Parks, 619/221-8901; San Diego Regional Parks, 619/531-1527; surf report, 619/221-8884

ACCOMMODATIONS

The rents on the bayfront are higher than those on the oceanfront, but the noise factor has to be considered. You do want to go to sleep eventually, right? We saw a cozy little cottage on the bay side that rented for $750 a month, but next door was a chic *Architectural Digest* centerfold that was going for closer to $750 a week. The scuttlebutt is that all the good, affordable ones are booked months, if not years, in advance, usually by people who faithfully return each summer. We can't blame them. For rentals in the area, contact **Discover Pacific Beach** (1503 Garnet Avenue, Suite 113, Pacific Beach, 858/273-3303).

This leaves motels, of which there aren't many in Mission Beach. The largest and best option is the **Catamaran Resort Hotel** (3999 Mission Boulevard, 858/488-1081, www.catamaranresort.com, $$$), with 313 units, many with bay views. There's a safe bay beach at the back, where you can rent sailboats and get windsurfing lessons, and there's a tropical pool on the premises. Things occasionally get hopping at the on-premises lounge, tastefully named the Cannibal Bar, if you're looking for a little après sail.

COASTAL CUISINE

As if to reinforce the twin themes of fun and nourishment, the best places to eat in Mission Beach are often the best places to drink, too. Our favorite is **Guava Beach Bar and Grill** (3714 Mission Boulevard, 858/488-6688, $$). With doelike innocence, the friendly waitresses at Guava Beach Bar hustle about, making small talk and refilling drinks within seconds of last sips. Most of the staples on the menu have a Mexican flavor, and all items are reasonably priced and perfectly unfancy.

Guava Beach offers "Baja Bargains" every day, happy-hour specials like the Cabo quesadilla with sour cream, spicy Rosarito fish taco, and brie and calypso salsa quesadilla.

The best antidote for the inevitable hangovers you will suffer in Mission Beach is **The Mission Café** (3795 Mission Boulevard, 858/488-9060, $), which is by general consensus the best breakfast place in the area.

NIGHTLIFE

There are two camps in Mission Beach's nightlife: those who are preparing to party and those who are already partying heartily. The prelude to a party animal's evening in Mission Beach is to watch the sunset from one of several Ocean Front Walk bars. The hottest one during our expedition was **'Canes** (3105 Ocean Front Walk, 858/488-1780). If you can find the roller coaster, you can find 'Canes, which practically sits in its shadow. Formerly one of the legendary Red Onion clubs and then a popular place called Chillers (we've imbibed at both incarnations), 'Canes carries on the tradition with live rock and roll. The club regularly brings in great national acts, too. We kicked ourselves for missing, by one day, an appearance by NOFX and Rancid, two of the more intelligent punk bands rattling the cage. 'Canes gets some serious competition for "party central" honors with **Wavehouse** (3125 Ocean Walk, 858/228-9283), which, in addition to wall-to-wall beach revelers, boasts a simulated wave called the Flowrider. Believe it.

The **Open Bar** (4302 Mission Boulevard, 858/270-3221) is one block off the beach, but equally popular with locals for preludes to serious partying. Ditto for the **Pennant** (2893 Mission Boulevard, 858/488-2223), at the south end of the peninsula. It is a sloppy hut with a wooden bar and booths, plastic cups of draft beer, and boisterous and sometimes slurred conversations.

Finally, we present one of our new favorites in all of Southern California: the **Liars' Club** (3844 Mission Boulevard, 858/488-2340). Its jukebox and draft beer selections have attracted a loyal local following. Most Mission Beachers who don't hunker down for the duration at one of these spots end up heading to the even more boisterous bars in Pacific Beach.

Mission Bay

Tucked behind the peninsula of Mission Beach, Mission Bay is a world unto itself and a beach haven that, though popular, remains nicely out of the way. The beaches here are on the bay, of course, and many visitors come to sail out on the water, not splash about the calm shoreline. This 4,600-acre aquatic park—the largest on the West Coast—can be accessed via numerous ramps, landings, and marinas to the north and west and on Fiesta Isle, the largest of the two fabricated islands in the bay itself. Watery activities pursued here include fishing, sailing, windsurfing, water-skiing, and swimming, and the sight of people doing all of these things at once gives the scenic and unpolluted bay a sort of relaxed elegance, not unlike a Seurat painting of a scene along the Seine.

Mission Bay is also a living lesson in democracy. Everyone comes here, from wealthy bon vivants, relaxing on deck in sailor suits and caps, to camping anglers, bunking in tents and RVs at the two campgrounds on the north shore. The bay is, in fact, appealing in so many ways that it's almost a shame it has to "compete" with the ocean beaches just a Frisbee toss to the west. But that only means there's plenty for everyone in San Diego.

From a tourist's standpoint, the centerpiece of Mission Bay Park is **SeaWorld** (500 Sea World Drive, 619/226-3901, www.seaworld .com). This 150-acre marine zoo stars Shamu (a two-ton killer whale), dolphins, otters, walruses, sharks, eels, and stingrays. There are also shark and penguin encounters, Dolphin Discovery, and Cirque de la Mer (Circus of the Sea). SeaWorld isn't cheap ($51 for kids 3–9, $71 for everyone else), but it's open

9 A.M.–11 P.M. in the summer (9 A.M.–dusk the rest of the year). If you hang out long enough you might get your money's worth.

For more information, contact the San Diego Visitor Information Center, 2688 East Mission Bay Drive, San Diego, CA 92109, 619/276-8200 or 800/422-4749, www.info sandiego.com.

BEACHES

They're not ocean beaches, but there's a bevy of sandy bay beaches to be found on **Vacation** and **Fiesta Islands,** as well as Mission Bay's mainland shoreline. Probably the best among half a dozen of them is to be found at **De Anza Cove,** on the bay's northeast flank. Here you'll find a well-equipped public park, as well as private campgrounds for tents and trailers.

ACCOMMODATIONS

Two excellent and affiliated RV campgrounds are available. Along Mission Bay, **De Anza Harbor Resort** (2727 De Anza Road, 858/581-4281, $), off North Mission Bay Drive, has 250 spaces for RVs ($39–45 per night, 858/273-3211). The much larger and more scenic **Campland on the Bay** (2211 Pacific Beach Drive, 858/581-4200, $) is a "premium RV resort" boasting 750 spaces for both tents ($40) and RVs ($67 per night). SeaWorld is right across the bay.

If you want more in the way of creature comforts, try the **San Diego Paradise Point Resort** (1404 West Vacation Road, 858/274-4630, www.paradisepoint.com, $$$) on Vacation Island in Mission Bay. It's stocked to the gills with everything you could possibly desire, including five pools, a golf course, and a bayside beach. Formerly the San Diego Princess Resort, the property has undergone several phases of renovation in recent years. The goal is to recapture its original charm, back when it was a "vacation village" conceived by a Hollywood producer turned resort developer back in 1962. Rates run $185 and up for a standard guest room.

COASTAL CUISINE

For dinner we ventured over to the San Diego Paradise Point Resort, on the smaller of two man-made isles in the heart of Mission Bay. In a setting of tropical gardens, **Baleen** (1404 West Vacation Road, 858/490-6363, $$$$) serves superb seafood-oriented cuisine, offering a dining experience that's tough to top in San Diego. Every table in the spacious and casually elegant dining room has a postcard-perfect view of the bay. Wood-roasted fish such as mahimahi and salmon are highly recommended. Just be forewarned that everything is à la carte, and you'll pay $30–35 per entrée, plus $6.50 for vegetable side dishes and $7 for desserts, accruing a very pricey tab on your culinary pleasure cruise.

Pacific Beach

Any beach town that names itself after the world's largest ocean better have the waves to back it up. Happily, Pacific Beach (or "P.B." as it is known to locals) has waves upon waves of great surf, great beaches, great weather, great bars, and great cheap eateries. In short, Pacific Beach (population 40,000) is the quintessential Southern California beach town and is among our favorites on either coast. Despite the occasional encounter with a shirtless drunk sporting a bad attitude, P.B. is still the place to go if you want to have serious fun in San Diego.

There is an unstated rivalry between Pacific Beach and La Jolla, the jewel on the hill four miles north. Natives have bemoaned the gentrification that has trickled down from their wealthier neighbor. They've mockingly dubbed themselves "Baja La Jolla" for all the rich preppies who come here to party. And, indeed, some overly trendy boutiques have muscled onto the scene in Pacific Beach. Still, it seems unlikely that any business that charges $32 for designer T-shirts is going to last long.

The irony about this give-and-take between the two towns is that P.B. itself, beyond the

BAD VIBES IN PACIFIC BEACH AFTER DARK

Southern Californians are unabashedly sensual. They are children of the sun, as Jim Morrison dubbed them, physically fit and mentally uncomplicated. The state of profligate fun that colors their every waking activity is played to an unending soundtrack of laughter and rock and roll, and they never seem to tire of each other's presence. This is never more evident than at night when they come out to play after a hard day of hanging out in the ever-shining sun.

On the surface the nocturnal rites of Southern California unfold in a relaxed and thoroughly appealing state of anarchy that somehow manages to stay within the bounds of civilized behavior most of the time. Perhaps this is simply due to the fact that every day is nearly perfect here, at least from the perspective of weather-beaten East Coasters like ourselves. Since tomorrow is a clean slate, it's no big deal if things don't work out today.

Southern Californians owe this sunny outlook to the fact that they are always engaged in some physical activity and therefore don't have time to develop the pathologies that haunt sedentary folks in other places. Of course, all this fun in the sun also leaves little time to develop the mind, beyond periodic dabbling in the latest New Age manifesto. Hey, if there's an awesome happy hour going on somewhere, who's got time to get serious? And, more important, who needs to?

If it all seems too good to be true, it is. The pressure of paradise produces its own pathologies. We saw this dark side rear its head one night in Pacific Beach. Actually, it was the Fourth of July, of all symbolic days, and the festivities had come to a begrudging end around 2 A.M., at which point a hungry contingent of beach bums descended on one of several Mexican fast-food outlets that stay open all night in P.B. We did likewise.

At the first taco hut we visited, a sad-comic scene ensued. While we studied the hand-lettered menu, a grocery cart entered from stage right, listing like a rusty galleon with a tall load of empty cans and Hefty bags. The cart was pushed by a sun-pulverized woman of indeterminate age, perhaps 35, perhaps 70. She was wearing a grease-stained miniskirt, fluorescent orange fanny pack, dirty knee socks, and torn, untied sneakers that were too small for her swollen feet. From out of the shadows staggered her consort: a shirtless, shoeless man with tattoos covering his bare, distended belly.

commercial corridors of Garnet Avenue and Mission Boulevard, is a well-tended, suburban, and relatively pricey place in which to live. That left us wondering where all the wasted Marky Mark look-alikes go at the end of the night. There must be a whole lotta house sharin' goin' on. We know for a fact there's a whole lotta shakin' goin' on in those shared houses, as a stroll down any Pacific Beach side street after dark will reveal. One night, while setting out for a round of Garnet Avenue pub-crawling, we parked in front of a house where beer, music, and conversation were flowing loudly from a second-story balcony. A young woman, oblivious to the fact that she was broadcasting her monologue to an entire city block, shamelessly recounted the previous night's drunken revelry to her male consorts.

You've gotta love the carefree mindset of the P.B. surfer dude. Late one afternoon, we popped into a drugstore for notebooks and drinks. The tanned surfer clerk at the front register didn't just point us to the proper aisle. This genial, sunny dude gave us a guided tour of the entire store! We learned more about his life in five minutes than a team of therapists would have gotten out of either of us in a week. He even complimented us on our choice of

He answered to "Bear," the name shouted by the woman as he stumbled across the street. She loudly begged Bear for a dollar, the modest sum needed to buy an order of rolled tacos. Bear growled and extended a paw, proffering a moist, wadded bill extracted from the unfathomable folds of his soiled jeans. While she approached the window to order, he proceeded to gruffly panhandle the other people in line. We left at that point, having witnessed more human pathos than we could stomach after a night of prowling among the Barbies and Kens of San Diego.

The second Mexican restaurant we visited provided a scene of actual mayhem that had only been hinted at by the first. After ordering quesadillas, we retreated to a corner booth, feeling bad for the man behind the counter. Before taking our order he had been verbally abused by a Surfer Joe-type who accused him, in mock Mexican dialect, of withholding the sour cream from his burrito. The place was as loud as the bar we'd just left; the revelry never seems to end in Pacific Beach.

We tried to enjoy our food, though the helpings were so large that they seemed to multiply like protoplasm with each bite. As we were finishing, an odd series of events took place. Like a row of dominos stood back to back, it only took one jolt to send them all tumbling down. The jolt was provided by a skateboarding local and his companion, a woman in overalls. Her mate took offense at something he heard in line. This ignited a bizarre scene that ended with an athletic man who was not even involved in the original dispute punching the woman wearing overalls so hard that her head hit the front window of the restaurant with a sickening thud. A college kid ran outside to break up the fight, during which a heavy trash can got overturned.

The collegian ended up getting pummeled, as did the skateboarder who'd set things off. After leaving the parking lot strewn with four prone, moaning bodies, the assailant took off down Garnet Avenue. The cops arrived at that point, trying to sort out something that had no rationale. The final grace note was provided by one of the original disputants, an oblivious guy in line whose chance remark had touched off the fracas. Exiting the restaurant with his takeout order, he surveyed the parking lot and exclaimed, "I started all this, and I didn't even get punched!"

The quesadillas weighed heavy on our stomachs as we rehashed this turn of events. In a way, we felt like we'd lost some of our innocence about Southern California. For all its paradisiacal trappings – and the day at the beach that was now ending had been one of the most perfect we've encountered – we detected an underlying dissatisfaction, the ennui of the pampered American psyche that wants more of everything: sex, money, power, sun, surf, and good times.

thirst-slaking beverages, proudly informing us that he had risen at 7 A.M. to stock that very drink refrigerator himself. As he was ringing us up, he sincerely offered us his best wishes. And we sincerely bade him the same.

On the way out, we passed a man entering the store. He was dressed in a toga, with a band of ivy tied around his head. He was not in a costume drama, as far as we could tell. Out in the parking lot, we came upon a classic Mutt-and-Jeff duo, P.B.-style: a short, shirtless, tattooed construction worker and a tall, gangly, long-haired dude on crutches. The guy with crutches was toting a 12-pack of Bud-

weiser, lightened by the brewskis the pair had already knocked back. They spied a woman coming out of the drugstore and stopped to admire her pulchritude. (There's nothing subtle about P.B. dudes with beer in them.) The woman, blond and surgically improved but no more attractive than 90 percent of the gals in P.B., climbed into her shiny black, vanity-plated SUV. Hobbling toward her, the dude on crutches urgently shouted, "Miss! Miss!" The woman rolled her window partway down, perhaps thinking there was something wrong with one of her tires. "You're sexy!" the guy on crutches blurted with a crooked grin. "There, I said it!" Then he hobbled away, giggling with his drinking buddy.

Two blocks away, on the boardwalk near Crystal Pier, two athletic California beauties were jogging side by side. After they passed a gaggle of guys, one gasped to the other, "Did you check out those dudes, dude?"

So it goes in P.B., dude, a party town without equal.

For more information, contact Discover Pacific Beach, 1503 Garnet Avenue, Pacific Beach, CA 92109, 858/273-3303, www.pacificbeach.org.

BEACHES

The main beach at Pacific Beach is part of a two-mile strand that extends south from Crystal Pier down to Mission Bay Channel. It is, quite simply, the most popular beach in San Diego and is jam-packed all summer long. Surfers in particular like **Pacific Beach,** rising with the sun to catch the early-morning waves. Areas for swimmers and surfers are marked off, to avoid confusion and collision. A cement walkway for strollers, runners, inline skaters, skateboarders, pets and owners, plus those who simply like to ogle the passing parade, links Pacific Beach and Mission Beach. A crew of San Diego city lifeguards surveys the scene at both beaches.

On the north side of Crystal Pier is **North Pacific Beach,** which runs for a mile up to Tourmaline Surfing Park in La Jolla. North Pacific Beach is a little narrower and rawer than the main beach strand—the cliffs begin to rise en route to La Jolla's curvaceous coves—and a bit less crowded as a result.

11 PACIFIC BEACH

    BEST (

Location: from Crystal Pier (Garnet Avenue and Mission Boulevard in Pacific Beach) south to Mission Beach
Parking/Fees: metered street parking
Hours: 4 A.M.-2 A.M.

Facilities: concessions, lifeguards, restrooms, showers
Contact: San Diego Coastline Parks, 619/221-8901; San Diego Regional Parks, 619/531-1527; surf report, 619/221-8884

12 NORTH PACIFIC BEACH

Location: from Crystal Pier (Garnet Avenue and Mission Boulevard) in Pacific Beach) north to Tourmaline Street in La Jolla
Parking/Fees: limited street parking
Hours: 4 A.M.-2 A.M.
Facilities: concessions, lifeguards, restrooms, showers
Contact: San Diego Coastline Parks, 619/221-8901; San Diego Regional Parks, 619/531-1527; surf report, 619/221-8884

ACCOMMODATIONS

The **Pacific Terrace Hotel** (610 Diamond Street, 858/581-3500, www.pacificterrace.com, $$$$) is the best place to stay in the area. The three-story pink and brown hotel blends as unobtrusively with the sand as a 73-room inn possibly can, and the location, just north of the Crystal Pier on the beach, is unsurpassable. Built on the site of what used to be a transient flophouse, the Pacific Terrace is a modern luxury hotel, comfortable and clean without being stuffy. Many of the rooms have balconies overlooking the ocean and the large heated pool. Purchased in 1989 by a large property management corporation, the Pacific Terrace has embraced some La Jollan affectations in recent years (valets in safari outfits), but no other place on the beach in San Diego can match it. However, with rooms starting at $260 a night in the summer, it is not for beach bums on a budget.

In contrast to the Pacific Terrace, the **Crystal Pier Motel** (4500 Ocean Boulevard, 858/483-6983, $) is more affordably priced. The name does not lie. It sits directly on the short, historic Crystal Pier (dating from 1927).

© PARKE PUTERBAUGH

Pacific Beach

The rooms are actually separate cottages affixed to both sides of the weather-beaten pier. Each cottage has a different sea creature carved into the cute blue shutters (in case you forget your room number, just remember "Sea Horse"), as well as an enviable pier-side private patio. The Crystal Pier Motel is popular with fishing families, members of which drop their lines into the water from their patios. It's not luxurious, but it is clean and unique.

COASTAL CUISINE

Restaurant-wise, P.B. is a battle royal between burgers, burritos, and fish 'n' chips, with no clear winner. Too many franchises have muscled their way onto the scene in recent years, but there is an alternative: buy the same fare from the locals. For example, the best burgers in town are served at **Cass Street Bar and Grill** (4612 Cass Street, 858/270-1320, $), which is also a great watering hole for locals, many of whom eat here so often it might as well be an extension of their refrigerators.

Close by, for seafood, try **The Fishery** (5040 Cass Street, 858/272-9985, $$$), where you can sit down beneath mounted fish and

dig into California swordfish piccata or cast-iron-blackened ahi. Mosey over to Thomas Avenue, where you'll find the **Green Flash** (701 Thomas Avenue, 858/270-7715, $$) and **Nick's at the Beach** (809 Thomas Avenue, 858/270-1730, $$). Beyond that, we've never seen a town so thick with taco shops, burger stands, bars, and other spots to duck into for quick, cheap bites.

NIGHTLIFE

In the immortal words of a local P.B. party animal, "For me there's living at the beach. Then there's middle age. And then there's death." Perhaps this deep philosophical musing best captures the transcendent wildness of the nightlife here. On our numerous visits to P.B., we've hung out at enough places to fill a scorecard and once even managed to get pulled over by the cops. We looked at it as a rite of passage.

The old reliables—**Cass Street Bar and Grill** (4612 Cass Street, 858/270-1320) and **Kahuna's Surf Bar** (873 Turquoise Street, 858/488-6201)—are still around. The latter is perhaps the ultimate unrefined surf bar on the

Southern California coast. As with the pipeline of a wave, only dauntless surfers venture inside. Surf music plays on the jukebox, longboards hang from the ceiling, surfing footage plays continuously on video monitors, and the place is packed with rowdies, especially on the "rage nights" of Friday and Saturday. When we last visited, the place was run by a scary-looking guy with a gray beard and baggy, soiled shorts. Throughout the evening he taunted and regaled the crowd over a microphone, offering free shots of tequila to any woman who'd bare her breasts for him, leaping over the bar to referee a fist-fight that he helped instigate, and leading cheers of "Kahuna! Kahuna! Kahuna!" as he paced behind the bar like a trapped panther.

Moondoggies (832 Garnet Avenue, 858/483-6550) is a tamer, trendier chain sports/surf bar that caters more to surfer wannabes. It's got comedy nights, deejay nights (one devoted to "industrial" music), and drink specials (like "Surfers on Acid"), and it's definitely not our style.

Two other old reliables on the P.B. scene are **Hennessey's Tavern** (4650 Mission Boulevard, 858/483-8847) and **Pacific Beach Bar and Grill** (860 Garnet Avenue, 858/272-4745). The former, though part of a chain, has been adopted by locals mainly because it occupies the site of a late, lamented Mexican cantina. The latter has an excellent jukebox, an outdoor patio, and a line out the door all night long. Year after year, it remains the most popular spot in town. There are generally more people waiting outside to get in here than there are partying inside at most other bars, so come early and grab a meal from the surprisingly voluminous and tasty menu. Try a Longboarder: corn tortillas stuffed with mahimahi, salsa fresca, and white sauce. The main dining room has long wooden tables with cheap plastic deck chairs at which you sit unabashedly with others, as if on a big indoor picnic, which makes for good and downright unavoidable mingling. On a recent visit, we were joined by six garrulous UCSD students who might've been even louder had they not been stuffing their faces so frantically.

The place with the longest lines and loudest crowds on our last cakewalk up Garnet Avenue was the **Typhoon Saloon** (1165 Garnet Avenue, 858/373-3444). Security personnel in yellow slickers self-importantly communicate with one another via walkie-talkie, and this "bad-ass" joint teems with noise and bodies on the move and on the make.

If dance music is your thing, try **Club Tremors** (860 Garnet Avenue, 858/272-7278), which shares an address and is associated with the infinitely more preferable Pacific Beach Bar and Grill. Like luscious lemmings who come to honor a monument to their own narcissism, guys and dolls crowd into Tremors on hot summer nights, primped and preened and mirror-conscious. Formerly the trendy Club Diego's, it's a massive multimedia complex. You must pay a cover to hear taped hip-hop music played at a volume that could scare off the gulls circling nearby. It certainly sent us fleeing. Similar deejay fare is offered at the tonier **Plan B** (945 Garnet Avenue, 858/483-9921), which nonetheless seems to attract a slightly seedier clientele.

If you're as averse to electronic dance music as we are, there are plenty of alternatives in Pacific Beach. Two of our favorites are **Plum Crazy Saloon** (1060 Garnet Avenue, 858/270-1212) and **Cafe Crema** (1001 Garnet Avenue, 858/273-3558). The former is an extremely friendly place, with good music, countless drink specials (68 beers on tap!), pool tables, and delirious locals, typified by a blond woman who pantomimed every song played, replete with pelvis and lip twitches and tabletop leg kicks. Cafe Crema is part of the coffeehouse craze, which has overtaken even beery Pacific Beach. Open 22 hours a day, Cafe Crema bakes its own pastries and offers an excellent array of rich coffees, plus treats like "Latte of the Month" and "Creme de la Crema" (44 ounces of espresso, ice cream, whipped cream, chocolate, and banana), as well as healthy soups and salads, and alcoholic beverages. Books and magazines are strewn about, card and chess games are in progress, and folk music is earnestly strummed. Last time we dropped in, a professorial duo delivered an earnest, academic seminar on acoustic blues. Most of the inattentive clientele was absorbed in novels, textbooks, and alternative newspapers. It was a Friday night, and all hell was breaking loose on the streets and in the darkened saloons of Pacific Beach. The well-lit Cafe Crema, by contrast, offered a civilized, if woozy, alternative to the alcohol-fueled festivities outside the picture windows.

Speaking of which, **Blind Melons** (710 Garnet Avenue, 858/483-7844) rocks P.B. with live music at the foot of Crystal Pier. Blues-rock seems to be the genre of choice at this corner bar, where we heard a Janis Joplin sound-alike going for broke one balmy weekend afternoon.

La Jolla

On May 3, 1987, the town of La Jolla celebrated its centennial. In its coverage of the event, the *La Jolla Light* recounted the glorious spring afternoon in 1887 when La Jolla came into being. The first line of the story said it all: "It could not have been a better day for selling real estate." It was boom time in California, and settlers scurried westward to join in the land grab. One historical account claims they were sold a false bill of goods: "The plots were touted as having water mains and convenient telephone and rail service, none of which was true." It didn't matter. The setting was so much like paradise, perched high above the ocean on tawny, pine-covered bluffs, that no one was about to quibble over phone lines.

La Jolla (pronounced la-HOY-a) means "the jewel" in Spanish. Indeed, La Jolla does look like a jewel—maybe the prize bauble on the marble-topped vanity of coastal California. Wealth is palpable, both in the natural bounty of a marvelous setting and the material prosperity evident in the cars residents drive, clothes they wear, houses they live in, and the shops that cater to their every caviar-like whim. They make their money hawking real estate and trading stocks, occupations that allow them to bask in a perfect environment, squired away in upscale, uphill semi-exclusivity. The tone is set by signs that welcome

© PARKE PUTERBAUGH

La Jolla Cove

TOP TEN THINGS TO DO ON THE FOURTH OF JULY

On our nation's birthday, this was listed on the blackboard by the lifeguard shack at La Jolla Cove:

10. Watch fireworks.
9. Drink a beer.
8. Look for a parking space.
7. Eat veggie burgers and tofu dogs.
6. Drink another beer.
5. Yell at the guy who "stole" your parking space.
4. Swim at the Cove.
3. Drink another beer.
2. Ask the lifeguard a question.
1. Feel very patriotic.

visitors with the warning, "No shouting within city limits."

Technically, La Jolla (population 42,800) is a "Community of San Diego," but in every imaginable way it is a world removed. The freeway cacophony of downtown San Diego is miles away. La Jolla is distanced by attitude and altitude from rabble-rousing Pacific Beach and Mission Beach. Every attempt is made to cultivate a village atmosphere. La Jollans boast of having a "significantly high standard of living." It is a community whose residents lead a life of sensory indulgence. They are impeccably attired. They appreciate good food, wine, and art. They are masters at landscaping. Their hair is perfect. And, like all busy people pursuing wealth and privilege in the new millennium, they often appear to be harried as they bustle around their little seaside sanctuary.

The corporate heart of La Jolla is the intersection of Prospect and Fay Streets, which looks like a bonsai version of Wall Street. Outside the offices of Paine Webber and Merrill Lynch are arrayed gleaming rows of Mercedes and BMWs—foreign-made cars for patriotic free-enterprise capitalists. The working women, who tend toward the real-estate professions, likewise fix their steely gazes on the pot of gold at the end of the corporate rainbow. We actu-

ally overheard a couple of them at a seaside café discussing, over lunch, the origin and meaning of the company name "Re/Max."

The men all look to be some indeterminate, forever-young age, resembling those perfectly coifed leading men on daytime-TV melodramas. They include gray-haired bon vivants driving racy red convertibles, consorting with blonde gold-diggers half their ages. We spied one younger, upwardly mobile professional, whose dirty-blond long hair was heavily moussed and neatly swept back, pecking furiously at a calculator while nursing a grande latte at the local Starbucks. We could imagine him, like a surfing Superman, changing out of his Clark Kent office attire into baggies and sandals, grabbing his board and making for the waves at Windansea when 5 P.M. rolled around.

The ocean exerts a near-mystical pull upon all who live in La Jolla. At day's end they gravitate to the ocean's edge, gazing over the broad expanse at the setting sun like Bedouins engaged in prayer rituals. They watch from porches and balconies. They pull up to curbs in cars and vans with surfboards jammed in back or tethered on top. They jog along Coast Boulevard. Some bring picnic baskets, crawling onto sandstone shelves to toast the rosy sun as it slides into the crystal goblet of the Pacific.

SURFER GIRLS

Surf Diva Surf School, in La Jolla Shores, was founded in 1996 by Isabelle ("Izzy") Tihanyi, a legendary surfer who has competed in professional tournaments, and her twin sister Coco. Among the things that the Tihanyis and their instructors teach are how to read waves; how to "pop up" (go from a horizontal to a vertical position, like a human jack-in-the-box); how to maintain proper knees-bent, arms-out standing position; how to paddle against the prodigious West Coast waves; how to maintain balance on the board; and, of course, how to safely take a spill.

Surf Diva is not for wimps. Surfing is strenuous exercise. As Tihanyi told one magazine, "An hour of surfing is equivalent to 200 push-ups, and if you catch fifty waves, it's like doing sprints all day long." Tihanyi also suggests that students be competent swimmers (able to swim 200 yards) and "be comfortable in the ocean."

Surf Diva charges $165 for a two-day weekend surfing clinic and $390.50 for a five-day clinic. They also have summer camps for kids (boys and girls). The school provides equipment (boards, wet suits, lines, etc.), but women should bring all other items they'd normally bring to the beach (sunscreen, swimsuit, towels, sunglasses, hat, bottled water, food). Preregistration is required.

For more information, contact Surf Diva, 2160 Avenida de la Playa, La Jolla, CA 92037, 858/454-8273, www.surfdiva.com.

The scene at sundown is emblematic of the Southern California experience. On one especially lovely late afternoon in midsummer, we set up camp at Windansea to watch the unfolding parade. Vans lined the street, their doors slid open to reveal fur-covered seats, carpeted floors, and knee-high card tables at which guys in cutoffs sat cross-legged, cracking jokes and sipping beer. A trio of divers with yellow tanks strapped to their backs waded into the water, caucusing briefly before disappearing beneath the surface. An apple-cheeked beauty with shiny blond hair jogged by wearing a turquoise sweatshirt and coral sweatpants. A surfer in a wet suit came sprinting down a side street, board tucked under one arm, anxiously scanning the waves. People assumed the lotus position on rock ledges, hands shielding eyes from the harsh glare of the dimming sun as they gazed seaward. A girl in a bulky sweater, guitar slung over a shoulder, sang, strummed, and strolled out onto the rocks as if serenading the sea. On the water a surfer caught an amazing ride, tunneling through the foam and down a sloping wave until he was shooting the curl. Moment by moment, the setting sun slowly turned the buff-colored sandstone to honey.

Despite its lofty perch, cracks in La Jolla's facade have periodically emerged, depending on the temper of the rocky markets. Prospect Street has seen a gradual incursion of less tony shops. In the midst of all the jewelers, perfumeries, and art galleries displaying Miró lithographs have come low-rent T-shirt stores and bargain rug merchants. Even McDonald's—designated a "McSnack" and mercifully lacking in golden arches—has stiff-armed its way onto a prime block of Prospect Street. We've seen panhandlers wandering the streets, a further blight to La Jolla's formerly unalloyed brilliance. One evening we followed the incongruous sound of banjo-picking to a downtown street corner, where a faux hillbilly whose hat lay upturned at his feet played bluegrass for the well-to-do Californians who strolled around him. On the street, a woman offered Tarot readings and on-the-spot counseling to those wandering by. She gazed deeply into the eyes of a customer, holding her hand while consulting

"DID YOU GIGGLE TOGETHER?"

The high-pressure lifestyle of making and spending money in volatile economic times is bound to take a toll that no amount of tennis or scuba diving can adequately soothe. This perhaps explains why La Jolla, a town of 40,000, lists 200 psychologists and psychiatrists in its Yellow Pages, not to mention the usual array of psychic problem-solvers (mediums, astrologers, fortune-tellers). Stress remains a hot topic of conversation. Signs of trouble in paradise are evident and even audible, as we discovered one afternoon. While strolling past a gorgeous estate in La Jolla, we heard its occupants screaming so loudly at each other that we thought the stucco was going to crack.

Relationships are casually psychoanalyzed down to the most intimate details. At dinner one night, we were seated near a medical professional and his date (whose occupation went undivulged). Both were in their early 40s, recently divorced, and talkative to the point of indiscretion. We certainly heard every word.

The male interrogated his partner with highly personal questions whose premises were profoundly silly. "Did you ever get to the point where you dug each other on a soul level, or was it all fantasy?" he earnestly queried. "Did you giggle together?" he asked with deep concern. By this time we were giggling together, heads buried in our plates so as not to draw attention. The conversation proceeded to a lengthy recounting of a humiliating tongue-lashing he'd received from a psychic nutritionist with whom he'd consulted. Despite his wounded ego, he generously interpreted her insults as "a loving gesture."

This recalls another true story, related to us by a former New Englander now living in suburban San Diego. He attempted to organize a reading circle. He explained the concept to his well-tanned but apparently poorly read neighbors, one of whom looked perplexed.

"You mean we read books and then sit around and talk about them?" he asked.

"Yes, that's the idea."

"Indoors?!"

the cards. We tried to read her lips; it looked like she was saying, "I can feel your pain."

Despite occasional signs of slippage along the fault line dividing haves and have-nots, La Jolla remains Southern California's premier ocean-resort community, possessing a setting as splendid as any on the coast.

For more information, contact the La Jolla Chamber of Commerce, 8602 La Jolla Shores Drive, La Jolla, CA 92037, 858/454-1444, www.lajolla.com.

BEACHES

The ruddy sandstone cliffs and caves of La Jolla are a perpetual work-in-progress. The humans who scamper along the sandy, erodable rocks overlooking the sea are unwittingly contributing as much to its sculpted form

as the force of the waves that batter it from below. The beaches of La Jolla are among the most varied and striking on the Southern California coast. A new discovery waits around every turn in La Jolla, be it a blufftop vista, a stairwell leading to a small, sandy cove beach, or a rocky tidepooling zone. In their geological undulations and scenic variety, La Jolla's beaches are comparable with up-coast Laguna Beach. Both are among our favorite stretches of coastline in all of California.

La Jolla's sandy procession starts from the south with **Tourmaline Surfing Park,** at the west end of Tourmaline Street along the border between Pacific Beach and La Jolla. Tourmaline Surfing Park is off-limits to swimmers but is nirvana to surfers. Waves here are notoriously large and break a good distance from shore. There are no sand beaches to speak of between Tourmaline Surfing Park and Windansea Park, but there is public access to the shoreline—and excellent opportunities for tidepooling—at **Bird Rock Beach.** This residential area features some of the most palatial homes and desirable real estate in La Jolla. Stairs leading to the rocky beach can be found at the foot of Bird Rock Avenue and at North Bird Rock Vista Point (on Camino de la Costa between Cresta and Corta Avenues).

La Jolla's beach bounty—and the more public parts of its coast—begin at Winamar Avenue and continue up to La Jolla Cove. A paved path at the end of Winamar Avenue leads to a small, sandy beach. This is the start of an impressive trio of beaches—**La Jolla Strand Park, Windansea Beach,** and **Marine Street Beach**—that collectively occupy about a mile of prime La Jolla coastline. The beaches are flatter, sandier, more expansive, and less dramatic than the ones up along Coast Boulevard. These in-town favorites draw sizable numbers of surfers, anglers, swimmers, and divers. As the fabled locale of Tom Wolfe's *Pump House Gang,* Windansea is legendary among Southern California's surf elite. The famous "pump house" itself is located at Gravilla Street and Neptune Place. The waves are equally impressive at La Jolla Strand Park and Marine Street Beach, offshore of which lie Big Rock and Horseshoe Reefs.

Along Coast Boulevard, from its southern intersection with Prospect Street up to Ellen Scripps Park and La Jolla Cove, are arrayed small beaches and inviting green spaces for swimming, sunning, surfing, and picnicking. The linear park along Coast Boulevard is equipped with benches and huts that people use for barbecues or as places to erect an easel and paint the coastal scenery. The seaside path along this stretch of coast is pure delight; we can scarcely imagine a better way to greet the morning or end the day. Our strategy is to park on Coast Boulevard (free street parking) and walk its length, resting on benches or lolling on grassy knolls every few hundred feet.

The coast vistas are among the finest in the world. Beach accesses along this enchanted strip commence with Nicholson Point Park, between the 100 and 200 blocks of Coast Boulevard, where a hard-to-find stairwell leads to a small, sandy cove. Next up are two small beaches known mainly to locals—**Whispering Sands Beach,** at the end of Bishop's Lane, and **Wipeout Beach,** south of Ellen Scripps Park on Coast Boulevard.

The crème de la crème of La Jolla's beaches is **Children's Pool Beach,** where Coast Boulevard meets Jenner Street. A breakwater curves out and around, protecting the beach's inner flank from waves and creating an ideal place to swim or sun. At least that's what the local harbor seals and sea lions think. They've appropriated Children's Pool Beach, while humans discreetly watch them doing nothing from the breakwater or bluff top. Waves slam the base of the breakwater, which has a walkway with a handrail from which one can survey the seals' and sea lions' laid-back version of beach blanket bingo. Sea spray from crashing waves sometimes soaks those standing on the breakwater, which can be refreshing on a hot day or a shivery nuisance on a cool one.

One summer afternoon we counted 44 sea mammals sunning themselves on Children's Pool Beach. Arrayed in the sand like fat sausages, they bark, cuddle, roll over, and occasionally shuffle and flop into the water for a cooling lap. Typically, they "haul out" of the water to relax and sun themselves for seven hours a day. They seem perfectly content to be around humans and their point-and-shoot cameras. Don't let your kids get too close, though. They are marine animals, capable of inflicting injury, no matter how "cute" they may appear. Nonetheless, it's a strikingly pleasant scene here all the way around.

Just north of Children's Pool Beach is **Ellen Scripps Park,** a bluff-top green that's perfect for picnicking, Frisbee tossing, or simply lying on your back and looking up at the sky. One Fourth of July, we saw people doing all those things and more. Vendors sell inexpensive, often

THE WORLD ACCORDING TO SURFER JEFF

We had just finished swimming laps and lifting weights at our hotel, thereby maintaining the Olympic stamina that allows us to keep pace with the tireless Southern California hordes after the sun goes down. Heading for the hot tub, we spotted a blond-haired lad. He turned out to be a surf bum in his mid-20s named Jeff. He hailed us as we approached, congratulating us for keeping in shape while handing over a couple of beers — lukewarm Bud Lights plucked from a 12-pack that was already more than half demolished. He was not a registered guest at the hotel, just a local who'd wandered onto the property to dangle his feet in the hot tub and knock back some brews.

His worldview was a mixture of hedonism and pathos, an outlook common to those who outwardly have it all yet inwardly feel a spiritual void. It is the subject behind just about every song the Eagles ever wrote, including "Hotel California," the ultimate hand-wringing anthem for conflicted hedonists. They talk like this only to make themselves feel less guilty for having so much fun. We refer to it as "sunny angst."

Surfer Jeff was the peroxide-blond embodiment of sunny angst. After handing us our beers, he struck up a friendly conversation. He wasted no time informing us, a pair of total strangers, that "it's time for me to get my life together." He paused, then confessed, "I'm getting old. I'm almost 25." He'd like to get out of La Jolla, he said. It's a town where "your life is everyone else's business," where people stab you in the back. He admitted to having family problems; his folks were less than thrilled that their high-school-dropout son was still perfecting his form on the waves but had no career prospects. In addition, he intimated that among the townsfolk he was widely regarded as a wastrel who'd worn out his welcome.

"I've got a bad reputation around here," he confessed. "I don't know why, but I do."

Outwardly, he was an exemplary specimen of young California manhood, neatly massaged to a lean, muscular turn by sun, wind, and waves. His skin had been bur-

environmentally themed T-shirts. Windswept trees form a canopy over the sidewalk, sculpted so that their limbs grow horizontally. A broad, brown band of kelp floats offshore. Those who are so inclined can stroll out onto a staircase of sandstone ledges and watch the sunset.

At the south end of Ellen Scripps Park, stairs lead to **Shell Beach,** a steep, sloping beach tucked into a small cove, whose coarse brown sand is evidence of a rough, high-energy surf zone. Shell Beach gets packed with sunbathers, but few venture beyond the point where the waves break. Just below Point La Jolla, at the west end of La Jolla Cove, is **Boomer Beach,** a popular spot for bodysurfing. Surfboards are forbidden because of dangerous rip currents.

The beach at **La Jolla Cove** is the most popular in the vicinity, and it's invariably choked with a thick tide of beach blankets and bodies at the height of summer. It is staffed by lifeguards who post jargon-filled daily swimming and diving conditions on a blackboard; e.g., "Surf: Picking up slightly 1–2' west with a southern component that is spuratically *(sic)* trying." During one of our visits in early July, the water temperature hit 69.2 degrees and the locals were exultant. To them this was bathwater, very close to the yearly high of 71 degrees, reached in August and September. Further cause for celebration was this note, posted on an information board near the lifeguard stand: "Ocean water testing at the cove and shore will be suspended until October. Results have shown that water off the cove is generally excellent during the summer and early fall months." In other words, you don't have nished to a ruddy brown, while his windblown hair bore the color of Midwestern hay. He positively glowed with the boisterous virility of a life lived outdoors. But now he found himself an unwilling adult with no career and no life beyond that of hanging ten and then guzzling at least that number once he'd climbed out of the water.

"I've got no tools," he lamented, holding up his hands as if to display his lack of real-world skills.

He possessed nothing beyond an ability to ride the waves and to party all night long. That may be all you need to get by while in the throes of a reckless California youth, but it won't pay the bills or feed a family. Not that he's got (or wants) a family or material goods, however forcefully they're urged on him by a culture that won't take no for an answer. In Surfer Jeff's world, who really needs anything more than a warm day, a nice southern swell, and a tall, cool brew?

We figured out that he's basically contented with his life, uttering remorseful monologues from time to time to convince others that he's "serious" about the future. In reality, his philosophy is like that of Henry Miller, who opened the novel *Tropic of Cancer* with these lines: "I have no money, no resources, no hopes. I am the happiest man alive."

Surfer Jeff recast that sentiment in his own words: "I've tried to get away, but the beach keeps calling me back. There's just something about it. It's so much fun that there's no real incentive to think of doing anything else. Just when you get bored with the whole scene, there's always somebody new who will wander down the beach with a cooler full of beer. It's like, 'Where's the next pool? Where's the next party? Where are we going now?'"

At this point a friend who waited tables in the hotel restaurant wandered into the pool area for a smoke. Surfer Jeff instantly switched out of his introspective mode and loudly greeted his buddy with a series of birdlike squawking noises. They slapped a mighty high-five, and the new arrival accepted the beer shoved at him, even though he was still on duty in a tuxedo. They talked about plans for later that evening. "If you come up with something to do," pleaded Surfer Jeff, "please drag my sorry ass along with you, man."

to worry about swimming in a soup of fecal coliform bacteria, as you might elsewhere in Southern California.

La Jolla Cove and Underwater Marine Reserve stretches in a broad, tongue-shaped curve from Ellen Scripps Park up to Scripps Pier, at which point the coast resumes its northwesterly course. The area has been designated an ecological reserve in which boats, spears, floats, dogs (between 9 A.M. and 6 P.M.), and glass are prohibited. The public beach at the west end of La Jolla Cove (by Ellen Scripps Park) is protected and calm, and therefore gets quite crowded. The cove itself fills with scuba divers, snorkelers, and long-distance swimmers, some of whom are well over 60. They make the chilly swim across the cove, emerging like amphibians at La Jolla Shores.

Then they shake themselves off until presentably drip-dried and hitchhike back to La Jolla, wearing only their Speedos. The locals know them on sight, so rides come easily.

Incidentally, another local attraction is the **Coast Walk,** a cliff-hugging and footbridge-crossing dirt path for the hale and hardy that begins above **La Jolla Caves** and proceeds about halfway toward La Jolla Shores. The caves lie 144 steps below the Coast Walk; both sights are worth the trouble.

The focal point of La Jolla Shores, a suburb northeast of La Jolla, is **La Jolla Shores Beach-Kellogg Park.** The mile-long beach is flat and the summer waves often gentle enough to make this a good family beach. Kellogg Park is a grassy picnic and play area behind the beach. Our first impression of La Jolla Shores

Beach–Kellogg Park, on one slamming summer day, was that it looked like a refugee camp. The sand was as thick as a bamboo jungle with people. Packs of children threw black-sand mudballs at one another and screamed as they braved the surf on the broad beach. La Jolla Shores Beach–Kellogg Park belongs to the people, and the people do indeed turn out to frolic on it. We've rarely seen a beach as crowded as this one, though it's calmer on weekdays and at other times of the year, as we've verified on subsequent visits.

One memorable year we ended a daylong Fourth of July ramble around town at Windansea. We wound up wandering out to the beach after demurring on a party to which some surfers had invited us. It had sounded promising: the waiter/surfer/college student who told us to come described life at his apartment complex, a few short strides from Windansea, as a nonstop episode of *Melrose Place.* Apparently, we came too late. By the time we arrived, it looked more like an episode of *Sanford and Son.* Trash cans full of empty beer cans and pizza boxes were already being dragged to the curb, and except for a rap record blaring in the apartment and a girl skating in the driveway, the party was over. We kept walking down Bonair Street till it ended at Windansea. Then we perched on a sandstone ledge, listening to the soothing sounds of the sea in the aftermath of the holiday fireworks. We've said it before and we'll say it again: California can be a paradise to rival any on earth.

13 TOURMALINE SURFING PARK

Location: west end of Tourmaline Street, at Chelsea Street and Crystal Drive, in La Jolla
Parking/Fees: free parking lot
Hours: 4 A.M.–2 A.M.
Facilities: lifeguards, restrooms, showers, and picnic area
Contact: San Diego Coastline Parks, 619/221-8901; surf report, 619/221-8884

14 BIRD ROCK BEACH

Location: in La Jolla at the end of Bird Rock Avenue
Parking/Fees: free street parking
Hours: 4 A.M.–2 A.M.
Facilities: none
Contact: San Diego Coastline Parks, 619/221-8901; surf report, 619/221-8884

15 LA JOLLA STRAND PARK

Location: in La Jolla at Neptune Place and Palomar Avenue
Parking/Fees: free street parking
Hours: 4 A.M.–2 A.M.
Facilities: none
Contact: San Diego Coastline Parks, 619/221-8901; surf report, 619/221-8884

16 WINDANSEA BEACH

Location: in La Jolla at Neptune Place and Bonair Street
Parking/Fees: free street parking
Hours: 4 A.M.–2 A.M.
Facilities: none
Contact: San Diego Coastline Parks, 619/221-8901; surf report, 619/221-8884

17 MARINE STREET BEACH

Location: in La Jolla at the end of Marine Street
Parking/Fees: free street parking
Hours: 4 A.M.–2 A.M.
Facilities: none
Contact: San Diego Coastline Parks, 619/221-8901; surf report, 619/221-8884

18 WHISPERING SANDS BEACH

Location: in La Jolla at the end of Bishop's Lane
Parking/Fees: free street parking
Hours: 4 A.M.-2 A.M.
Facilities: none
Contact: San Diego Coastline Parks,
619/221-8901; surf report, 619/221-8884

19 WIPEOUT BEACH

Location: in La Jolla on Coast Boulevard
Parking/Fees: free street parking
Hours: 4 A.M.-2 A.M.
Facilities: none
Contact: San Diego Coastline Parks,
619/221-8901; surf report, 619/221-8884

20 CHILDREN'S POOL BEACH

Location: in La Jolla at Coast Boulevard and Jenner Street
Parking/Fees: free and metered street parking
Hours: 4 A.M.-2 A.M.
Facilities: lifeguards
Contact: San Diego Coastline Parks,
619/221-8901; surf report, 619/221-8884

21 SHELL BEACH

Location: base of stairwell at south end of Ellen Scripps Park (Coast Boulevard at Girard Avenue) in La Jolla
Parking/Fees: free and metered street parking
Hours: 4 A.M.-2 A.M.
Facilities: lifeguards and restrooms
Contact: San Diego Coastline Parks,
619/221-8901; surf report, 619/221-8884

22 BOOMER BEACH

Location: south end of La Jolla Cove, reachable from Ellen Scripps Park (Coast Boulevard at Girard Avenue) in La Jolla
Parking/Fees: free and metered street parking
Hours: 4 A.M.-2 A.M.
Facilities: lifeguards and restrooms
Contact: San Diego Coastline Parks,
619/221-8901; surf report, 619/221-8884

Children's Pool Beach

23 LA JOLLA COVE

BEST (

Location: in La Jolla at Coast Boulevard and Girard Avenue
Parking/Fees: free and metered street parking
Hours: 4 A.M.-2 A.M.
Facilities: lifeguards and restrooms
Contact: San Diego Coastline Parks, 619/221-8901; surf report, 619/221-8884

24 LA JOLLA SHORES BEACH-KELLOGG PARK

Location: in La Jolla Shores at Camino Del Oro and Calle Frescota
Parking/Fees: metered parking lots
Hours: 4 A.M.-2 A.M.
Facilities: lifeguards, restrooms, showers, picnic tables, and fire pits
Contact: San Diego Coastline Parks, 619/221-8901; surf report, 619/221-8884

ACCOMMODATIONS

The inns and hotels of La Jolla tend to be on the sumptuous (read: expensive) side, so don't come here looking for budget Best Westerns. The nicest are the European-style hotels downtown and overlooking the cove. Our pick of the litter is the **Grande Colonial Hotel** (910 Prospect Street, 858/454-2181, www.thegrandecolonial.com, $$$$), a well-appointed hostelry that dates from 1913. Rooms are plush, and amenities include a heated pool in a gorgeous courtyard and free valet parking. You'll pay anywhere from $225 for a standard village view room to $365 for a deluxe ocean view. Then there's the lavishly appointed **La Valencia** (1132 Prospect Street, 858/454-0771, www.lavalencia.com, $$$$), a salmon-colored stucco wonder that looks and feels like "old California," if not the Old World. This "luxury destination resort" charges some mad money here: $275 for a "petite room," $350 for an ocean view, $525 for a King deluxe, with

suites going to up to $1,050 and the La Valencia Suite going for $3,500—per night. You could buy a decent surfboard for one night's stay here! In any case, the beaches of La Jolla are just steps away out the back doors of the Colonial Inn and La Valencia.

Even closer is **La Jolla Cove Suites** (1155 Coast Boulevard, 858/459-2621, www.lajolla cove.com, $$$), a four-story modern structure that trades what it lacks in architectural distinction for a prime location directly overlooking La Jolla Cove and a few steps away from Ellen Scripps Park. Oceanfront balconies, heated pool, and proximity to La Jolla's downtown shopping district are added pluses. Rooms run $170–250; suites are more expensive.

Another of the fancy in-town hotels, the **Empress Hotel of La Jolla** (7766 Fay Avenue, 858/454-3001, www.empress-hotel .com, $$$), swaddles its guests with old-world elegance and contemporary luxury. Large, comfortable rooms are appointed with marble-tiled baths, well-stocked minibars, and terrycloth robes that hang inside mirrored closet doors. Mauve cloth napkins are placed next to a gilt-edged ice bucket. (You get the idea.) On the lobby level is a gourmet Italian restaurant called **Manhattan;** in the basement, an exercise room, spa, sauna, and showers. Rooms are surprisingly affordable; in the summer of 2008, a room for two was going for $199–225—a bargain by La Jolla standards.

Being partial to beachside locations, we've found the **La Jolla Shores Hotel** (8110 Camino Del Oro, 858/459-8271, www.ljshores hotel.com, $$$$) to be the best combination of location and comfort in the area. Formerly the Sea Lodge, its 128 rooms surround a tropical-plant-filled terra-cotta courtyard. All rooms have balconies or lanais, and La Jolla Shores Beach–Kellogg Park is literally steps away. The feeling out here is more outdoorsy, rustic, and recreational than it is in La Jolla's business district. With its arched, wood-plank ceilings, it feels more like a ski lodge than a sea lodge—until you sniff the salt air blowing off the ocean. Recreational facilities include a heated outdoor pool and tennis courts; the hotel also will provide guests with beach equipment, such as chairs, umbrellas, and volleyball equipment. It's highly recommended—and very expensive ($350 and up, in season). To help defray some of the travel expense, the hotel is offering gas cards and "free parking for hybrid vehicles," though we'd just prefer they drop the room rates and not charge for parking.

The **Hotel La Jolla at the Shores** (7955 La Jolla Shores Drive, 858/459-0541, www .hotellajolla.com, $$$) is a modern, 11-story high-rise four blocks from La Jolla Shores Beach–Kellogg Park. In addition to panoramic ocean views from the recently renovated rooms, the Hotel La Jolla boasts a world-class restaurant, **Crescent Shores Grill** (858/459-0541, $$$), on its top floor. The menu is oriented toward California/American cuisine: steak, seafood, pasta, and good wines. In-season rates at the hotel run $169 and up.

Finally, for corporate chain partisans, the 400-room **Hilton La Jolla Torrey Pines** (10950 North Torrey Pines Road, 858/558-1500, $$$$) overlooks the ocean and sits next to a golf course. A perfectly adequate and reasonably priced **Radisson Hotel** (3299 Holiday Court, 858/453-5500, $$) reposes in the hills west of town center, where I-5 meets La Jolla Village Drive.

COASTAL CUISINE

La Jolla's restaurant scene is dominated by **George's at the Cove** (1250 Prospect Street, 858/454-4244, $$$), a three-story restaurant that offers diners the option of semiformal indoor dining downstairs or a more casual setting on an outdoor deck that overlooks La Jolla Cove. On a midsummer evening, we took the latter option, enjoying the extensive view out to sea and up the coast. We dined on grilled marinated swordfish and a mixed grill of three fish, both of which were absolutely delicious. The third-level deck looks out on the ocean as if from the bow of a ship. Plexiglas panes keep the wind at bay, and heat lamps provide a note of warmth to counter the chill. Yes, we were

dining on the beach in Southern California in July and heat lamps were needed. There's a pronounced fall-like tang in the air even in midsummer along the California coast, thanks to the ocean's giant cooling engine.

Downstairs, the more formal dining room at George's specializes in creative seafood preparations done with a California flair—e.g., apple-smoked salmon served with fennel, miso, and Hawaiian pesto; and halibut in chicken fumet with poached leeks, garlic, and shallots. George himself can be seen bustling around the premises, impeccably attired and super-competent, yet possessing a dry, seen-it-all wit reminiscent of John Cleese. George's at the Cove is a La Jolla landmark and a must-try for visitors.

On the Mexican side you'll find decent sit-down Spanish and Mexican restaurants along Prospect Street, such as **Jose's Court Room** (1037 Prospect Street, 858/454-7655).

Overlooking the water near La Jolla Cove is **Brockton Villa** (1235 Coast Boulevard, 858/454-7393, $$$). This historic, restored "red rooster" beach cottage gained a second lease on life as a popular breakfast and lunch spot. (It also serves dinner now.) A favorite dish is chicken curry with jasmine rice. We dug into a delicious Moroccan halibut salad and pulled pork quesadilla after a long hike around La Jolla's curvy, majestic shoreline on as perfect a day as you could ever hope to find.

La Jolla's dining scene is rich and varied enough to reward serendipitous browsing. We had an excellent late lunch at **Bollicine** (8008 Girard Avenue, 858/454-2222, $$$). It's a great multilevel Italian restaurant and martini bar just up the hill from La Jolla Cove. Bubbling water tanks are shaped like martini glasses. The restaurant's main emphasis is salmon, prepared in all sorts of ways. Try the riso salmon entree (chunks of fish in riso pasta with a side of penne—simple but good) or a salmon sandwich on focaccia. Have a salmon lunch or dinner with a martini to wash it down and you'll be thanking us for the tip.

Tapanade (7612 Fay Avenue, 858/551-7500, $$$) is a relatively recent arrival (1998).

A nice but not too fancy place, Tapanade has an excellent, unpretentious menu inspired by the Provence region of France. Be sure to try the wild mushroom ravioli.

Pannikin Coffee (7458 Girard Avenue, 858/454-6365, $) has been around since 1968. It's great to sip coffee or Mexican hot chocolate on the patio.

NIGHTLIFE

La Jolla has steadily been losing some of its stuffy air, which has helped liven up its formerly stultifying nightlife. Today the multilevel mini-malls of Prospect Street contain the likes of a **Hard Rock Cafe** (909 Prospect Street, 858/454-5101) and **Moondoggies** (909 Prospect Street, 858/454-9664), one of a small but growing chain of spacious, upscale surf bars (find the oxymoron). However, in our judgment **Jose's Court Room** (1037 Prospect Street, 858/454-7655) is the place to go. A combination Mexican restaurant and bar, it was by far the liveliest joint we encountered in La Jolla. A loud CD jukebox sprayed its decibels upon a throbbing, three-deep crowd of beautiful people surrounding the oval island of the bar. The Mexican grub is good, but folks (especially singles) really crowd in for the company. So call out for an ice-cold Pacifico and join in the brew-ha-ha.

It's always a good idea to check what's on at the **La Jolla Playhouse** (2910 Village Drive, 858/550-1070), which was founded over 50 years ago by Gregory Peck, Dorothy McGuire, and Mel Ferrer.

Scripps Beach

A few miles north of La Jolla lies Scripps Beach. It belongs to the University of California at San Diego Scripps Institution of Oceanography (SIO), which maintains research facilities here. People generally come to Scripps to tour the Birch Aquarium, which is the most public of its facilities.

For more information, contact Scripps Institution of Oceanography, 9500 Gilman Drive, La Jolla, CA 92093, 858/534-3624, www.sio.ucsd.edu.

BEACHES

At **Scripps Beach** you'll find a research pier; offshore is a rocky reef and submarine canyon. While the beach here is sandy, it's not really appropriate as a place to come with the typical beach pursuits in mind. Therefore, if you're looking for a beach to frolic on, you're better off heading down to La Jolla Shores or up to Black's Beach/Torrey Pines State Beach.

25 SCRIPPS BEACH

Location: 0.6 miles north of Scripps Institution of Oceanography. From La Jolla Shores, proceed north on La Jolla Shores Drive for one mile. Turn left on El Paseo Grande and right on Discovery Way.
Parking/Fees: metered parking lots after 5 P.M. weekdays, holidays, and weekends; very limited street parking before 5 P.M. weekdays
Hours: 4 A.M.-2 A.M.
Facilities: none
Contact: Scripps Institution of Oceanography, 858/534-3624

Black's Beach and Torrey Pines State Beach

Before we hit the beach, let's spend a moment looking down on it from **Torrey Pines State Reserve.** One of the gems of the state park

THE SCRIPPS INSTITUTION OF OCEANOGRAPHY

The Scripps Institution of Oceanography is one of the oldest centers for marine research in the world. It was founded as an independent research lab in 1903 by a UC Berkeley biology professor and christened the Scripps Institution for Biological Research in 1912 for its benefactors, Ellen Browning Scripps and E. W. Scripps. Over time it focused its research efforts on the sea – an evolution that was recognized in 1925 when it was renamed the Scripps Institution of Oceanography.

The institution's assets include a fleet of four oceanographic vessels and two research platforms, classrooms and laboratories, shoreline and underwater reserves, seismological observatory and satellite oceanography facility, pier and aquarium/bookstore, major marine sciences library, and faculty and staff numbering more than 1,000. At any given time there may be 250 research programs underway, ranging from beach erosion to the physiology of invertebrates. If studying oceanography, marine biology, or earth science interests you, Scripps is the place to go for graduate training.

Even if doctoral studies in the geomorphology of ocean basins or manganese-nodule formation is not in your future, Scripps still has something to offer: the **Birch Aquarium at Scripps,** which is open to the public 9 A.M.–5 P.M. daily. Admission is $11 for adults and $7.50 for children ages 3-17. The Birch Aquarium and Ellen Browning Scripps Memorial Pier are in La Jolla Shores, just up from La Jolla Shores Beach–Kellogg Park.

The aquarium's glass tanks might contain everything from a spiny lobster to a gray grouper. Highlights include rainbow-colored exotics from Micronesia and the frozen-in-glass coelacanth, a nearly extinct relic from an ancient biological regime that looks like a battered piece of luggage. As a museum attached to a university-funded research facility, it's not quite as oriented to public visitation as the Monterey Bay Aquarium. But Scripps does offer a squid's-eye view of everything from kelp beds to coral reefs to the "Wonders of Water," plus a sense of the important research being conducted at the institution.

On that last note we'd like to lob this bit of wisdom at our readers, copied years ago from one of the exhibits, as we've seen evidence of its truth on every coast we've traveled: "Man has interfered with nature's supply of sand to our beaches, thus compounding the erosion problem, and we are now seeing the results of this intervention. Putting it bluntly, we are losing our beaches."

Scripps, however, is not losing its beach. In fact, Scripps Beach and the surrounding tidepools offer a wonderful way to learn about coastal ecosystems. It's all part of the Scripps Shoreline Underwater Reserve.

For more information, contact the Scripps Institution of Oceanography, 9500 Gilman Drive, La Jolla, CA 92037, 858/534-3624; or the Stephen Birch Aquarium Museum, 2300 Expedition Way, La Jolla, CA 92037, 858/534-3474, www.aqua.ucsd.edu.

© PARKE PUTERBAUGH

Torrey Pines State Beach

system, the reserve occupies a setting so peaceful you'll easily forget it brushes against a city of over a million. Trails lead into stands of the rare, long-needled Torrey pine, which grows only in this park and on Santa Rosa Island, 175 miles to the northwest. A 1.6-mile hike leads out to **Razor Point,** a breathtaking overlook from atop a 300-foot bluff. On a clear day, you can view the swell-dappled surface of the Pacific Ocean to the distant horizon. An old lodge, dating from 1902, serves as a visitors center. Some 436 plant and animal species are native to the park, including 144 birds, 110 invertebrates, 85 plants, 39 mammals, 28 reptiles, 23 fish, and seven amphibians.

In addition to its flora, fauna, and spectacular geology, the reserve is rich in fossils, and is close to where archeologists discovered the bones of Del Mar Man, believed to be the oldest human remains yet discovered in North America. The tranquility of the park is interrupted only by rustling breezes and the occasional sight of a gopher breaking open a Hottentot fig. The park offers a truly all-natural remedy for urban stress: an oasis of calm set beneath an awesome canopy of *Pinus torreyana.* On weekends, ranger-led walks are conducted at 10:30 A.M. and 2 P.M. It's

a very peaceful place to commune with nature and one of the better spots for coastal hiking in Southern California.

For more information, contact Torrey Pines State Reserve and Torrey Pines State Beach, 858/755-2063, www. parks.ca.gov.

BEACHES

The shore below Torrey Pines is **Black's Beach,** probably the most infamous nude beach in the country, and **Torrey Pines State Beach.** This lengthy strand lies at the base of the tall bluffs between Scripps Pier and Los Penasquitos Lagoon, and is as controversial as it is hard to reach. It is so out of the way we wonder why anyone would bother to get uptight about people enjoying the sun, surf, and sand in the buff. Yet the dimensions of the feud have occasionally plunged Black's Beach into the national news. Nudity was banned on Black's Beach in 1977, when a voter referendum revoked the "clothing optional" status. However, nudity has been the unofficial norm since then at Black's Beach. It is now official to the extent that an area of the beach—roughly between the Glider Part to the south and Mussel Rocks to the north—has been parceled off for nudists and marked with signs to that effect. Since July 7, 1999, the city's anti-nudity municipal code has been enforced on the southernmost section of Black's Beach, from Scripps Pier north for about seven-tenths of a mile. The fine for nudity outside of the marked area is $135, and for lewd conduct it's much worse. In other words, no lewd conduct. Got that?

From our perspective, the concern over nudity is grossly overstated. On a sparkling June afternoon some years back—Mother's Day, as fate would have it—all we saw were half a dozen men wandering the beach wearing only white socks and tennis shoes. On a warm afternoon in mid-July several years ago, the sum total of bathers in the buff consisted of an overweight couple of AARP age and several bearded male loners. We saw scant public nudity on Black's Beach on a balmy May weekend. Though we hiked till our feet hurt, we saw nothing but the occasional solitary bare-assed male. We did see lots of families, some picnicking on blankets. This gave the lie to the general impression of Black's Beach as America's premier nude beach.

In case you're curious, we were finally able to decode the putative partitioning of who disrobes where along Black Beach's two-mile stretch, thanks to a gatekeeper at Torrey Pines. Here's the lowdown: the north end is for men, the middle part is coed, and the south end is for surfers. "It's our Hawaii," said the gatekeeper, whose attention had to be pried away from a pod of dolphins whose offshore movements he was monitoring with a pair of binoculars. A surfer himself, he added: "The waves are good all over the coast, but for some reason they're particularly big down there." That is because a near-shore submarine canyon amplifies the swell, creating waves twice the height of others in the area.

The walk down to and along Black's Beach from Torrey Pines State Beach is one of the great environmental beach hikes in America. It includes a perilous scuttle around a point of land, called Flatrock, into which the merest sliver of a foothold has been carved into the rock. It is impassable at high tide. The geology of Torrey Pines and Black's Beach is an awesome spectacle. The sandstone cliffs are fascinatingly textured and colored with bands of red, yellow, and orange. Boulders and mounds of talus occasionally lie at the base of the cliffs. You might see an environmental artist creating human figures from rocks. We watched one tireless soul, who had created several dozen such sculptures for passersby to enjoy. Obviously, he could not sell or take them home. He was simply motivated by a compulsion to create something from the formless mounds of rock. The little figures did seem to have lifelike qualities, as if he'd created a village of hobbits from the variously shaped stones he stacked and arrayed.

Getting to Black's Beach is actually easier from above. A stairway descends from the Glider Port (off Scenic Torrey Pines Road). Steeply etched into the cliffs, this point of entry comes with a warning: Stairway and Cliffs Unsafe and Unstable. The warning goes unheeded, and the foot of the staircase roughly demarcates the surfer's zone from the coed nudists' encampment. The safest way down, however, is via the service road that begins where Blackgold and La Jolla Farms Roads meet. You can't drive a car down to it, but your own two feet will deposit you on the beach in 10 minutes or so. Free on-street parking is available, and there are a sufficient number of spaces (with two-hour limits) to handle demand most of the time, summer weekends and holidays excepted. The road to the beach drops steeply in a series of switchbacks, passing warning signs (Danger: Hazardous Cliffs Subject to Landslide) and irreverent graffiti (Do Not Eat or Feed Nudists) before depositing walkers onto the south end of Black's Beach, with Scripps Pier in plain view.

For our money, though, we prefer the longer, ground-level hike south from Torrey Pines State Beach, which offers a Kodak carousel's worth of dramatic slide-worthy scenery: enormous toppled boulders, giant talus piles at the base of the towering cliffs, and huge sheets of blackboard-smooth rock. The whole landscape has a wild, otherworldly appearance, which no painter can capture and no photograph does

© PARKE PUTERBAUGH

Black's Beach

justice. You simply must see it for yourself. Hikers should keep a watchful eye on incoming tides, which could potentially strand the unwary in a cove.

The less adventurous or ambulatory may prefer to stay put near the parking lots at Torrey Pines State Beach, a day-use beach. An ample parking area abuts Los Penasquitos Lagoon. Arrive early if you want a parking spot on a good beach day. Just be aware that the cobble-filled beach is inferior to the sandy, scenic, and less crowded expanses of Black's Beach. Our advice: Take a hike!

26 BLACK'S BEACH (A.K.A. TORREY PINES CITY BEACH)

Location: Hike down to the beach via the steep, gated, paved path that begins at the junction of La Jolla Farms Road and Blackgold Road in La Jolla. Or walk north along the beach from Scripps Pier or south from Torrey Pines State Beach.

Parking/Fees: limited free street parking on La Jolla Farms Road; $8 entrance fee at Torrey Pines State Beach

Hours: 4 A.M.–2 A.M.

Facilities: none

Contact: San Diego Coastline Parks, 619/221-8901; surf report, 619/221-8884

27 TORREY PINES STATE BEACH

Location: in Torrey Pines. Take the Carmel Valley Road exit off I-5, five miles north of La Jolla. Turn onto McGonigle Road and follow it to the beach.

Parking/Fees: $8 entrance fee per vehicle, or free along U.S. 101 6 A.M.–11 P.M.

Hours: 8 A.M.–sunset; visitors center, 6 A.M.–6 P.M.

Facilities: lifeguards, restrooms, and picnic tables

Contact: Torrey Pines State Beach, 858/755-2063

Del Mar

The never-ending boutiquing of Southern California reaches a modest crescendo in Del Mar (population 4,400). Del Mar is a trendy, buzzing little hive in town and a jazzed-up mall-o-drama out by its famous racetrack. The pace of traffic has picked up, giving Camino Del Mar a taste of the fumy, bumper-to-bumper backup that congests Laguna Beach. That's not to say the place has lost its charm, just that it's experiencing growing pains. But this is par for the coast; there's scarcely an available acre within sight of water in Southern California that hasn't been built up or targeted for development.

All the same, Del Mar is the closest you will come to finding a true village atmosphere in coastal San Diego County. Thanks to the vigilant attempts of the populace to keep development under control, coupled with the relaxed atmosphere of the beach and racetrack, Del Mar has the air of a less harried time in California's past. To a great extent, it has geography to thank. Del Mar is on a hill between two lagoons, with a canyon to the east and ocean to the west. If you're entering town from the east, a heart-stopping plunge down Del Mar Heights Road lets you know you're nearing the water. During our travels for this edition, Del Mar is where we began our coastal trek. When we came over the crest of the hill and saw the Pacific Ocean laid out before us, sighs of contentment at this auspicious sight simultaneously issued from our lips.

The land thins to precipitous strips at the lagoons: Los Penasquitos to the south (at Torrey Pines State Reserve) and San Dieguito behind and around the river mouth at the north end of town. There's only so much you can build out here that hasn't already been constructed or attempted. In the mid-1980s environmental prerogatives saved the San Dieguito Lagoon from plans to construct a cluster of hotels, shops, and freeway access ramps.

In town the only major project that's survived the legal gauntlet has been **L'Auberge Del Mar,** a $45 million luxury hotel and spa built on the site of the old Del Mar Hotel (which was demolished in 1967). Even so, it took the developer, a Del Mar resident, more than a decade to gain approval of the plan. The heart of the village, along Camino Del Mar from about Sixth to 15th Streets, is a cavalcade of small shops catering to a consumer's every whim. Folks mosey from cafés to shops, grazing and browsing, as traffic moves in fits and starts along Camino Del Mar while drivers scour the streets for parking spaces. The modest town center is a tasteful smattering of New Age shops (Earth Song Books), classy cantinas (El Fuego), and restaurants of long standing (Bully's North). Away from the main drag, Del Mar's blocks are filled with small but smartly designed trophy homes with amazingly landscaped lots on which every square foot is maximized.

The town is best known for the thoroughbred racing season at the **Del Mar Thoroughbred Club.** The brief, 43-day season runs from late July to early September, packing the town with racing buffs. The racetrack was built in the 1930s as the brainchild of local celebrities Bing Crosby, Jimmy Durante, and Pat O'Brien. Their cosponsor in the venture was the Works Progress Administration, which pulled out midway through construction. The celebs were left holding the bag, having to borrow funds to bring the track to completion. Crosby wrote and recorded a song to commemorate the track's opening in 1937. "Where the Surf Meets the Turf" is still played before the first race with all the dewy-eyed sentimentality of "My Old Kentucky Home" at Churchill Downs. The track lies inside a triangle formed by Via de la Valle, Camino Del Mar, and Jimmy Durante Way. The grounds are also the site of the annual **Del Mar Fair,** a June/July to-do that draws three-quarters of a million San Diegans. The rest of the year is given over to horse shows, trade shows, and concerts.

Before the first ". . . and they're off!" echoed around the track, Del Mar was already trotting along on an initially shaky but eventually well-heeled course. In 1883 developer Jacob Taylor Shell bought the strip of coastline upon which Del Mar sits today. He built a seaside spa on his 338 acres that included the Casa Del Mar Hotel, a dance pavilion, a bathhouse and pool, and a railroad depot. It briefly thrived before succumbing to bankruptcy, flood, and fire (in that order) by 1890. The town received a facelift during the roaring '20s: a renovated hotel, rebuilt pier, and new roads into town. The fairgrounds came in 1936, the racetrack a year later. Del Mar has grown slowly but steadily ever since, trying its best to remain—as a *Newsweek* article described it nearly 30 years ago—"a sleepy little seacoast town."

For more information, contact Del Mar Regional Chamber of Commerce, 1104 Camino Del Mar, Del Mar, CA 92014, 858/755-4844, www.delmarchamber.org.

BEACHES

Del Mar City Beach was a sunbather's paradise, quickly filling to capacity on summer days until 1998's winter storms nearly washed it away. It has since been "renourished" as part of an ongoing and expensive beach restoration project in northern San Diego County. Short concrete seawalls offer scant protection to homes that have been built too close to the water's edge. The high tide line, marked by seaweed and scalloped wave lines, runs up to the very base of the seawalls, which does not bode well for the future.

Even so, there is much to commend the beach at Del Mar, which widens as one nears the bridge over San Dieguito Lagoon. The main beach area has been subdivided into areas for different activities, with arrows delineating "Surfing and Beach Games" from "No Surfing and Beach Games." The south end of the beach has gone to the dogs, with leashed and unleashed canines chasing tennis balls into the water and romping around the sand. Many folks come here with their animal companions, so this might not be the best stretch of sand for sunbathing unless you're really into wet noses and sandy pawprints.

Finding a spot to lie out on the beach is less of a problem than finding a place to park close by. There's on-street metered parking along Coast Boulevard and a few pay lots. The early bird gets the parking spot while the loser cruises; parking in the summer months is pure hell. The beach itself is great for swimming and bodysurfing.

A grassy play area, **Seagrove Park,** sits on the short bluffs overlooking the beach from the south end. Del Mar's green bluff-top park is reminiscent of the village greens that are a mainstay of New England towns. On a sunny weekend afternoon—and few of them aren't sunny—students from UCSD, picnicking families, joggers, bicyclists, and walkers pack the park and its walkways.

Del Mar Bluffs City Park is just north of Del Mar City Beach, across the mouth of the San Dieguito River, where the land begins to rise again. A small sand beach here is popular with fishers. A steep wooden staircase laden with sand leads to a spectacular overlook from the top of the bluff. The panorama encompasses the ocean, racetrack, and town. Straddling Del Mar and neighboring Solana Beach is **Del Mar Shores,** a sandy stretch reachable from a tiny municipal parking lot at Del Mar Shores Terrace. These beaches are popular with locals and tourists alike, not the least reason being that in season you might catch trainers working their horses on the beach. Skin diving and surf casting are also popular here.

28 DEL MAR CITY BEACH

Location: in Del Mar at the west end of Camino Del Mar and 15th Street
Parking/Fees: metered parking lot
Hours: 24 hours
Facilities: lifeguards, restrooms, and showers
Contact: Del Mar Community Services, 858/755-1524

29 DEL MAR SHORES

Location: Del Mar Shores Terrace at South Sierra Avenue in Solana Beach
Parking/Fees: free street parking and free parking lots
Hours: 6 A.M.-10 P.M.
Facilities: lifeguards (seasonal)
Contact: Solana Beach Department of Marine Safety, 858/755-1569

ACCOMMODATIONS

Some things never change. **Del Mar Motel on the Beach** (1702 Coast Boulevard, 858/755-1534, www.delmarmotelonthebeach.com, $$) is where it's always been: smack dab on the beach. A charmingly unpretentious place that's been around since 1946, it's the only place in the area that can make that claim. The rates are much friendlier off-season ($139–179) than in the summer ($259–279).

Such homey motels are more the exception than the rule, as Del Mar and other North Coast communities are more typically represented these days by places like **L'Auberge Del Mar** (1540 Camino Del Mar, 858/259-1515, www.laubergedelmar.com, $$$$). You'll pay through the nose to be pampered at this resort spa. Visitors can select seaweed body packs, aromatherapy, reflexology, Shiatsu massage, and the ever-popular Balneo Therapy Revitalizing Bath from a menu of spa services more extensive than the list of ice cream flavors at Ben & Jerry's. It's a splendid resort, to be sure, with beautiful interiors, inviting pool area, multilevel decks, and walkways that meander among walled-in gardens that suggest a place far removed from the reality of a busy street corner. Large and well-landscaped grounds confer that all-important sense of splendid isolation that justifies room rates that run $200–385 in season (and around $700–800 a night for suites).

We are partial to the **Best Western Stratford Inn of Del Mar** (710 Camino Del Mar, 858/755-1501 or 888/478-7829, $$),

within walking distance of town but burrowed into a hillside in a real neighborhood. Constructed of gray, weathered wood, the Stratford Inn blends nicely into its environment. The grounds are invitingly quiet, featuring two heated pools.

COASTAL CUISINE

Down by Del Mar City Beach, a pair of restaurants with picture-window views of the ocean do a brisk business. **Jake's Del Mar** (1660 Coast Boulevard, 858/755-2002, $$$) and the **Poseidon Restaurant** (1670 Coast Boulevard, 858/755-9345, $$$) are the places to go if you want to dine by the water. Jake's offers a more imaginative menu of seafood prepared with a creative, Pacific Rim–style orientation, such as sesame-seared ahi with dark soy honey glaze. The Pacific seafood chowder (with fish, clams, and diced veggies) is rated among the best on the coast. The Poseidon sticks more closely to baked or broiled seafood basics. Both restaurants are overpriced—the cheapest entrée at Jake's, for instance, is $16, and the general range is $18–23—but you're paying not only for food but location, ambience, and a bit of history. The Poseidon has an especially inviting modern interior of varnished pine walls, tile floors, and big panoramic windows facing the ocean. It is a "view" restaurant offering breakfast, lunch, and a seafood-themed dinner menu.

The toast of the waterfront these days is **Pacifica Del Mar** (1555 Camino del Mar, 858/792-0476, $$$$). It is the best restaurant in town. You can't go wrong with choices like barbecued sugar-spiced salmon, which is the signature dish on a Pacific Rim–themed menu.

The **Fish Market** (640 Via De La Valle, 858/755-2277, $$) is an unpretentious, bustling sure bet for fresh seafood. If you're in a quandary about what to order, walk up to the fresh-fish counter, decide what looks good to you, and order it back at your table. The market smokes its own fish—the salmon/albacore combo is a must-try appetizer. Fresh fish entrées range from Utah rainbow trout to local thresher shark, plus skewers of scallops, oysters, ahi, and more. The Fish Market is close to the racetrack.

A good choice in town is **Carlos & Annie's Cafe** (1454 Camino Del Mar, 858/755-4601, $$), a Southwestern-themed restaurant that regularly wins "best breakfast" awards on the strength of such offerings as Carlos' Omelet (chicken, salsa, avocado, cheese, and Spanish sauce). On the other side of the street, **Cafe Del Mar** (1247 Camino Del Mar, 858/481-1133, $$) serves brick-oven pizza and creative pasta dishes, such as sautéed salmon with dill vodka sauce over penne, all priced very reasonably.

NIGHTLIFE

Generally, the night moves made in Del Mar are the sort of stretching and yawning calisthenics performed immediately before crawling into bed. As in most professedly quiet towns, there's not much to do beyond eating well, strolling a few blocks through the village after dinner, or maybe downing a highball at L'Auberge Del Mar to the polite accompaniment of a tinkling piano. You might find a little action in the bar at **Bully's North** (1404 Camino Del Mar, 858/755-1660), a prime-rib palace with an outdoor patio that's open till midnight. Otherwise, if you want nightlife you'll just have to roll up to Solana Beach, which has plenty of it.

Solana Beach

Solana Beach's claim to fame has been as party headquarters for north San Diego County. The townsfolk, whose per capita income of $65,000 per year is said to be even greater than that of Del Mar, haven't exactly been thrilled that their community has been the one to play Pied Piper to a hip-hopping party crowd. They've been working to change their image with tighter permitting and more vigilant law enforcement. As a result the nightlife has gradually become more evenly spread around this end of the county, spilling into Cardiff and up into Carlsbad. Ultimately, northern San Diego County is one big seaside overflow valve for the city of San Diego, 25 miles to the south.

Solana Beach (population 13,000) calls itself "the best spot under the sun." It's got two miles of beach, a number of decent restaurants and delis, and the Belly Up Tavern, one of the best live-music clubs in the country. In the past decade, Solana Beach has become a trendier spot, with splashy architectural and landscaping statements being made by hip entrepreneurs who've gravitated here. The San Diego Freeway (I-5) splits the town into east and west halves. U.S. 101 is the coast road in these parts, and this is where the town lets its hair down.

On an odd note, Solana Beach was the home base of the Heaven's Gate religious cult, whose members committed group suicide in March 1997. Economically, they fit the profile of the area. Mostly young, they designed websites for a living. They wore Nike tennis shoes ("just do it") the night 39 of them made their attempted afterlife rendezvous with a comet.

For more information, contact the Solana Beach Chamber of Commerce, 210 West Plaza Street, Solana Beach, CA 92075, 858/755-4775, www.solanabeachchamber.com; or San Diego North Convention & Visitors Bureau, 360 North Escondido Boulevard, Escondido, CA 92025, 760/745-4741 or 800/848-3336, www.sandiegonorth.com.

BEACHES

Access to Solana Beach's beaches is blocked, to a great degree, by residential housing. However, you can get through at **Seascape Surf Park,** accessible from the 500 block of South Sierra Avenue. A half mile north, Sierra Avenue meets Lomas Santa Fe Boulevard, dumping traffic into a large free parking lot at Fletcher Cove.

The coastal park in Solana Beach—we hesitate to call it a beach—is **Fletcher Cove Park.** It's an attractive natural setting, especially from the bluff-top vista point, which looks out over the pretty but fragile cliffs to the churning ocean below. The cove was blasted into being by early settlers, who dynamited the cliff bases. Obviously, environmental regulations would prohibit such a knuckleheaded move now.

Not surprisingly, there is no longer a beach at Fletcher Cove Park. It was devastated by a series of El Niño's (especially in 1998), and they trucked in sand from Yuma, Arizona, to raise the beach by six feet. That washed away, too, so now there's just the newly built park, complete with artificial turf. The beach is gone and the grass is fake, so you can draw your own conclusions. Ours aren't so favorable.

A half mile farther north is **Tide Beach Park.** At the base of a bluff reachable by a stairway, it's good for tidepooling, spear fishing, surf casting, and scuba diving. Nearly all of Tide Beach Park was lost in the winter of 1998, and subsequent renourishment projects have replaced sand with pebbles, making barefooting nearly impossible. The reef here is known as Table Tops. It makes for striking scenery but a bummer of a swimming beach.

30 SEASCAPE SURF PARK

Location: stairwell at 500 block of South Sierra Avenue in Solana Beach
Parking/Fees: free parking lot and street parking
Hours: 6 A.M.-10 P.M.
Facilities: lifeguards (seasonal) and showers
Contact: Solana Beach Department of Marine Safety, 858/755-1569

31 FLETCHER COVE PARK

Location: 111 South Sierra Avenue in Solana Beach
Parking/Fees: free parking lot
Hours: 6 A.M.-10 P.M.

Facilities: lifeguards, restrooms, showers, and picnic tables
Contact: Solana Beach Department of Marine Safety, 858/755-1569

32 TIDE BEACH PARK

Location: Pacific Avenue and Solana Vista Drive in Solana Beach
Parking/Fees: free street parking
Hours: 6 A.M.-10 P.M.
Facilities: lifeguards (seasonal) and showers
Contact: Solana Beach Department of Marine Safety, 858/755-1569

ACCOMMODATIONS

Solana Beach isn't exactly geared toward the tourist trade. The best choices are franchises: the **Courtyard by Marriott Solana Beach** (717 South U.S. 101, 858/792-8200, $$) and **Holiday Inn Express** (621 South U.S. 101, 858/350-0111, $$). Both are clean, attractive hotels within walking distance of the beach.

COASTAL CUISINE

A hip hangout on the relatively starved Solana Beach dining scene is **Pacific Coast Grill** (437 South U.S. 101, 858/794-4632, $$$). Diners can bring their dogs and sit on the garden patio (thereby obviating the need for a doggie bag). A good spread of Mexican food can be had at **Fidel's** (749 Genevieve Street, 858/755-5292, $$), a crowded cantina with an unpretentious atmosphere.

NIGHTLIFE

The **Belly Up Tavern** (143 South Cedros Avenue, 858/481-9022) enjoys a national reputation and is beloved by musicians and music fans alike. A roomy club, it is typical of other well-run, similarly sized nightclubs around the country that provide a living to musicians who might otherwise be applying for unemployment benefits. These include ghosts of the 1960s who have gone from stardom to cult status, as well as current up-and-comers. One night we caught a droll, low-key set by Dan Hicks, the San Francisco scene pioneer and gypsy jazz-pop stylist whose justifiably cynical disenchantment with the music business made for entertaining between-song patter.

Roots-oriented journeymen like Dave Alvin and Jorma Kaukonen and bluesy jam bands like the Radiators, along with a hefty number of reggae and R&B acts, fill the calendar at the Belly Up. The acoustics are great throughout, and the whole operation is first-class. Note that you must be 21 or older to come here. Some years back the club added a bistro-style restaurant next door, the **Wild Note Cafe** (143 South Cedros Avenue, 858/720-9000). The food is affordable, healthy, and hearty, while the music tends toward singer/songwriters and light jazz and funk. One duo name we'll never forget: Bongo and John. Check the Belly Up Tavern's website (www.bellyup.com) for concert schedules.

Cardiff-by-the-Sea

Cardiff-by-the-Sea takes its name from the Welsh seaport city. It is the most unassuming of the north San Diego County beach towns. The only industry that Cardiff (population 11,800) ever had dates back to 1912—a kelp-processing operation that closed three years later. Its chief attractions are the quiet residential neighborhoods east of U.S. 101 and two state beaches located opposite lagoons one at each end of town. Most of Cardiff lies uphill and east of the beach and railroad tracks. Given the condition of the beaches, these residents are no doubt glad they don't own beachfront property. Technically, Cardiff-by-the-Sea is part of the City of Encinitas, having participated in a four-in-one municipal conjoining back in 1986. In reality, the town has its own identity crisis. The identity is low-key, and the crisis is ruined beaches.

For more information, contact the Cardiff-by-the-Sea Chamber of Commerce, 2013 San Elijo Avenue, Cardiff-by-the-Sea, CA 92007, 760/436-0431, www.cardiffbythesea.org; or San Diego North Convention & Visitors Bureau, 360 North Escondido Boulevard, Escondido, CA 92025, 760/745-4741 or 800/848-3336, www.sandiegonorth.com.

BEACHES

Cardiff State Beach lies west of San Elijo Lagoon, separated from it by Old U.S. 101. The beach was once great for swimming, windsurfing, board surfing, and surf casting, but nearly all of the beach and the sidewalk and fencing behind it are gone, victims of a succession of El Niño years and winter storms. Cardiff is among the most severely impacted beaches in California. It is hard to describe the devastation, except to say that the scene is one of cataclysm. The parking lots are rutted and narrowed, the collection kiosks abandoned. The chain-link fences are listing, having absorbed repeated poundings from an ocean that has sent the beach into retreat—except there's no place to retreat, because of the seaside parking lots, restaurants, and highway. It is a disaster area, pure and simple, with gouged chunks of concrete and rusted metal skeletons littering the landscape in mute testimony to the ocean's might.

San Elijo State Beach is best known for camping, being the southernmost developed campground in the state system. Set high atop a jagged cliff, San Elijo's 171 sites fill up quickly. Reserve early, especially for the summer months. The campground is nicely laid out, with scraggly hedges providing some shade and privacy. The sites closest to the cliff's edge are the best. From these spots you can hear the waves crashing at night. You're also closer to the wooden stairs that lead to the beach. It is a long, lifeguarded beach and a good place to savor a gorgeous California sunset. The ongoing problem is that the narrowing campground has been pinned between a rock (U.S. 101) and a sandy place (the eroding beach). There's been talk of rerouting the channel connecting the lagoon and ocean so that it doesn't run on a beach-paralleling north-south route, which wreaks havoc on the bluffs and beach at Cardiff-by-the-Sea. A countervailing argument might go that the natural erosion of bluffs provides the very sand that replenishes these beaches, so it's probably the highway that ought to be moved.

To the east is the **San Elijo Lagoon Ecological Reserve**, a 1,000-acre wildlife haven that is one of the last wetlands of this size and purity in Southern California. Thanks to local activists, not only are the wetlands saved from developers, but the lagoon is accessible to hikers and bird-watchers.

33 CARDIFF STATE BEACH

Location: one mile south of Cardiff-by-the-Sea along Old U.S. 101 at San Elijo Lagoon
Parking/Fees: $8 entrance fee per vehicle
Hours: dawn to dusk
Facilities: none
Contact: San Elijo State Beach, 760/753-5091

34 SAN ELIJO STATE BEACH

Location: Cardiff-by-the-Sea along Old U.S. 101 at Chesterfield Drive
Parking/Fees: $8 entrance fee per vehicle; camping fees for sites on the ocean $39-44 per night with hookups, $30-35 per night without hookups, plus $7.50 reservation fee; inland campsites $10 less per night
Hours: dawn to dusk
Facilities: lifeguards, restrooms, showers, and picnic tables
Contact: San Elijo State Beach, 760/753-5091

ACCOMMODATIONS

If camping in the sand at San Elijo State Beach is too rustic for your taste, try the **Countryside Inn** (1661 Villa Cardiff Drive, 760/944-0427, $$). It's a 102-room Colonial-style hotel, once independent but now part of the Comfort Inn chain, with bed-and-breakfast amenities. One of the more striking constructions along this stretch of coast is **Cardiff by the Sea Lodge** (142 Chesterfield Drive, 760/944-6474, $$$). With its themed rooms, circular architecture, and rooftop fire pit for sunset savoring, this 17-room lodge makes a cozy romantic hideaway for couples.

COASTAL CUISINE

Cardiff has its own beachside "restaurant row" along Old U.S. 101. The place to dine is the **Beach House** (2530 South U.S. 101, 760/753-1321, $$$), a pricey, glitzy seafood restaurant so close to the beach the fish could practically swim from the ocean to the broiler. A rock revetment is all that stands between restaurant and waves. The parking lot attests to its popularity, as an army of young valets in tennis shorts and monogrammed pullovers take turns running the 40-yard dash, car keys jangling, to park or retrieve vehicles. The ocean views are fantastic, so try to come at sunset.

Next door, **Charlie's by the Sea** (2526 South U.S. 101, 760/942-1300, $$$) forthrightly advertises "any closer and you'd be wet." In truth, any closer and it'll be closed, as Charlie's by the Sea looks more like Charlie's *in* the Sea. The stylistically varied menu offers such entrées as macadamia-dusted scallops, sesame-seared salmon, and sea bass stuffed with smoked lobster and crab. Again, the picture windows look out on the vast churning ocean and the boulders that protect the restaurant from its fury.

Another neighbor on Cardiff's restaurant row is the **Chart House** (2588 South U.S. 101, 760/436-3751, $$$). It's part of a chain that serves excellent and inventive seafood dishes (sesame-crusted salmon, grilled tuna with mango relish) from choice ocean-view locations. If you miss it here, there are Chart Houses in Coronado, La Jolla, Oceanside, and Malibu, all of which have unsurpassable ocean views. Try to wrangle a window table, because the sights are as good as the edibles. Avoid the valet fee at the Chart House and Beach House by parking alongside U.S. 101 for free.

NIGHTLIFE

The **Kraken Bar & Restaurant** (2531 South U.S. 101, 760/436-6483) bills itself as "the bar by the beach...where the locals still and probably always will party." It has pool tables, pinball machines, and six color TVs. Summer happy hour runs 4 P.M.–7 P.M.

Encinitas and Leucadia

In 1986, Encinitas became a municipality made up of four formerly autonomous towns: Encinitas, Leucadia, Cardiff-by-the-Sea, and Olivenhain. Their conjoining is mainly a governmental matter. Olivenhain is rural and inland, while Cardiff stands apart from the others by virtue of geography. Encinitas and Leucadia, however, do seem joined at the hip—with the emphasis on hip, for these are two of San Diego County's most swinging coastal communities.

Encinitas is bounded at the south and north by the San Elijo and Batiquitos lagoons. The town is subdivided into "Historic Encinitas"—the area along U.S. 101, near the beaches—and "New Encinitas," along El Camino Real. The town's main problem is beach erosion. For years it's been fighting to save its beaches and ocean-front real estate. At one time there were Sixth and Fifth Streets in Encinitas. They do not exist now, having been annexed (so to speak) by the Pacific Ocean. A local geologist, using old surveys and maps, has determined that 800 feet of Encinitas's shoreline has disappeared in the last hundred years. The cliffs are made of sandstone, shale, and siltstone. Constant assault by waves opens cracks and fissures that eventually cause the cliff tops to pitch forward. Some coastal access points have washed out, and their precipitous stairwells are off-limits.

This is not to say Encinitas's beachfront does not have appeal. Despite the obstacles, the beaches are popular, primarily with teenagers (many from inland communities). Occasionally they exhibit threatening behavior and upset residents who have been coming here for years. The biggest story in town during one visit concerned "drunken abuse" taking place along the stairwell to Stone Steps Beach, where beer-drinking slackers were trying to intimidate families into leaving "their" beach, forcing them to join the crowds down at Moonlight Beach.

One of our favorite places in downtown Encinitas is **La Paloma Theater** (471 South U.S. 101, 760/436-5774). A slice of Southern California's socio-cultural past, this funky old single-screen movie palace dates from 1927. Today, it hosts everything from rock bands to first-run films to independent flicks. Spirit, one of California's greatest rock groups—led by the late, lamented Randy California—recorded a live album here. It's the sort of place where the latest surfing documentary is accorded the same fanfare that a new James Bond flick receives in Los Angeles. If you can believe it, they still show *The Rocky Horror Picture Show* on Fridays at midnight.

Another must-see attraction in Encinitas is **Quail Botanical Gardens** (230 Quail Gardens Drive, 619/436-3036, www.qbgardens .org). It's a 30-acre collection of plants and trees native to California, as well as exotic tropicals, palms, and bamboos. Visitors can take a self-guided tour of the premises, which includes a chaparral grove, a bird sanctuary, and more than 5,000 species of botanical life. Several of the many exotic environments include Africa, New Zealand, and the Canary Islands. Admission is $10 for adults and $5 for children 3–12, and it's open 9 A.M.–5 P.M. daily year-round. Interestingly, in the hills surrounding Encinitas, a thriving nursery and greenhouse industry grows most of the carnations dyed and sold on city streets around the world.

Leucadia is welded to Encinitas at a point where the latter's strip malls give way to unmoored (that is, un-malled) businesses, some of which look one season away from bank-

SELF-REALIZATION FELLOWSHIP HERMITAGE AND MEDITATION GARDENS

The most intriguing spot in Encinitas is a place of worship. The 17-acre grounds of the Self-Realization Fellowship Hermitage and Meditation Gardens (215 K Street, Encinitas, 760/753-2888) cling to the cliffs at the southern end of town. The nearby **Self-Realization Fellowship Temple** (939 Second Street, Encinitas, 760/436-7220) is visually dominated by three towers that loom above U.S. 101 like an exotic hallucination. The lotus towers were designed by Paramahansa Yogananda (1893-1952), the spiritual leader who founded the center in 1937 and built the temple in 1938. At the time, it was the largest building on the Southern California coast.

Yogananda dedicated his life to uniting East and West through the ancient art of meditation. He lived in the hermitage for several years and helped design the cliff-side meditation gardens. He planted the ancient ming tree on the site of his favorite pond, which was drained when the cliffs collapsed in 1941. Yogananda made a name for himself internationally with his *Autobiography of a Yogi,* which he completed here in 1946. It is now considered a classic of spiritual literature. The lively, detailed text traces the spiritual awakening of this gentle man, whose teachings profoundly affected the lives of many Westerners, including Greta Garbo, Leopold Stokowski, and Christopher Isherwood.

The best indication of Yogananda's spiritual openness is that his retreat and gardens have always been open to visitors. You are free to stroll and meditate to your heart's content, with no attempts at proselytizing. The meditation gardens are open for visitation Tuesday–Saturday 9 A.M.-5 P.M. and Sunday 11 A.M.-5 P.M. The nearby temple is open daily (except Monday) for meditation and prayer noon–4 P.M. Incidentally, the gardens are just steps away from a great beach (Swami's) and an eatery called **Swami's Cafe** (1163 South Highway 101, 760/944-0612, $$), specializing in smoothies and "whole foods."

ruptcy. Founded by English spiritualists in 1888, Leucadia lies along a congenial, tree-lined, and slightly run-down stretch of U.S. 101 that parallels the crumbling sea cliffs. Leucadia retains a bit more of an alternative flavor than Encinitas. It's the kind of place where New Age vegans, old-guard hippies, and dying VW bugs go to roost. The town that time forgot, Leucadia seems happily stuck in a tie-dyed mindset that feels more like the 1960s than the new millennium.

We like it here, as they've managed to keep heavy-handed developmental imperatives at bay. Instead you'll find small, nonfranchised businesses from taco shops to smoothie stands, from psychics to espresso bars, from greenhouses to New Agey places with names like The Energy Within. Eucalyptus trees line the road, and a homey, naturalistic ambience is exuded. A huge hill separates the road and town from the beach. Turn west off the highway onto any side street and you'll climb up and then dipsy-doodle down toward the beach.

Leucadia means "Isle of Paradise" in Greek, and the streets here are named for Greek deities (Daphne, Diana, Phoebe, Glaucus). But as in the Elysian Fields, not much goes on here. The number-one industry appears to be the selling of used merchandise, with a disproportionate number of businesses along U.S. 101 involved in the secondhand trade (thrift shops, consignments, used clothing, etc.). Our favorite was a yellow U-Haul on whose sides was inscribed an offer to buy used blue jeans 10 A.M.–3 P.M. on Sundays. A roadside motel called the Ocean Inn is not on the ocean at all,

SURF WRITERS

Because of their good surf, hidden coves, and relative affordability, Encinitas and Leucadia are popular with surfers, especially older ones with the means to live on the coast. Among the best known is Chris Ahrens, the publisher of the now-defunct *Longboarder* magazine and author of a book of true surf stories called *Good Things Love Water*. It's a sympathetic, if somewhat sentimental, collection of tall tales and profiles. One surfer described it as "someone standing around a fire ring talking with other surfers."

Longboarder magazine, back issues of which are fetching collectors' prices on the Internet, shared space on the magazine rack with *The Surfer's Journal, Longboard Magazine* (both based in San Clemente), *Surfer,* and others. Ahrens on the surfer's raison d'être: "Once you're out in the water, the rules of the land are left behind. A whole new government takes place. It's a kind of peaceful anarchy." (Or maybe not so peaceful: Plenty of bloodshed over territory and waves rights occur on California's choicest wave-riding beaches.)

Other surf writers of distinction include Greg Noll, whose *Da Bull: Life Over the Edge* is this legend's oral history, generally regarded as the best book about surfing in existence. Mike Doyle, a surfing legend in his own right, has published a memoir called *Morning Glass,* which captures the halcyon days of surfing. The diary-like entries are written chronologically and make a good historical reference tool.

We can't resist commenting on *The Pump House Gang,* Tom Wolfe's 1966 attempt to capture the manners and mores of a group of surf bums who made their home on the beaches of La Jolla. His sneering portrait is universally reviled by surfers. Here is an excerpt: "Their backs look like some kind of salmon-colored porcelain shells. They were staring out to sea like Phrygian sacristans looking for a sign.... I foresaw the day when the California coastline would be littered with the bodies of aged and abandoned Surferkinder, like so many beached whales."

Here is a hand-picked selection of books on the subject of surfers and surfing:

- *All for a Few Perfect Waves: The Audacious Life and Legend of Rebel Surfer Miki Dora,* by David Rensin. Gripping bio of legendary surfer/con man and self-proclaimed "King of Malibu."

- *Book of Waves,* by Drew Kampion.

- *California Coastal Access Guide* (Berkeley: University of California Press, 6th edition, 2003). This resource guide provides definitive information, in written and tabular form, on every publicly accessible beach. Changes from one edition to another are so minor that, unlike this book, each new edition is really more like a reprinting.

- *California Surfriders,* by John Heath "Doc" Ball. First published in 1946 and now reprinted, this pictorial record of "thrills, spills, personalities, and places of California surfing" was lovingly put together by Doc Ball, the first professional surf photographer.

- *Caught Inside: A Surfer's Year on the California Coast,* by Daniel Duane. An episodic, readable account of a guy who spent a year chasing waves. He doesn't sugarcoat the surfing life – some of the characters he befriends are deplorable – which makes the book all the more authentic.

- *Complete Guide to Surfing,* by Peter L. Dixon. Part history but mostly how-to, it's a good, contemporary (published in 2001) addition to the surf-book shelf.

- *Cowabunga!: A History of Surfing,* by Lee Wardlaw. Although not as definitive as *Surfing: The Ultimate Pleasure,* it has its charms.

- *Girl in the Curl: A Century of Women in Surfing,* by Andrea Gabbard. The fairer sex takes its turn in the lineup.

- *Hawaiian Surfriders 1935,* by Tom Blake. This is the first book ever written on the history of the sport. The author is the inventor of the paddle board, and a surfing legend in his own right.

- *Learning Hawaiian Surfing: A Royal Sport at Waikiki Beach, Honolulu, 1907,* by Jack London. Yes, this is *the* Jack London, who learned the sport in the summer of 1907 from the great George Freeth.

- *Let's Go, Let's Go! The Biography of Lorrin "Whitey" Harrison: California's Legendary Surf Pioneer,* by Rosie Harrison Clark.

- *Photo/Stoner,* by Matt Warshaw and Jeff Divine. The chronicle of Ron Stoner, who in the mid-1960s was generally regarded as the best surfing photographer. His images, in fact, helped define the sport in the mind's eye of young Americans, an innocent idyll before condominiums aesthetically ruined America's coastlines. At the peak of his fame and talent, Stoner disappeared, lost to drugs and madness. This book sympathetically captures his lost art and his precipitous fall.

- *Stoked: A History of Surf Culture,* by Drew Kampion.

- *Surf Rage: A Surfer's Guide to Turning Negatives into Positives.* The author, Nat Young, wrote this book after being assaulted while trying to surf his home break. He is to be commended for bringing the darker side of surfing to light. We hope it does some good.

- *Surf Science: An Introduction to Waves for Surfing,* by Tony Butt. Surfing meets physics and oceanography, and the attentive wave-rider is the winner.

- *Surfer's Start-Up: A Beginner's Guide to Surfing,* by Doug Werner. An easy-to-read and best-selling how-to guide. Warner also wrote *Longboarder's Start-up: A Guide to Longboard Surfing.*

- *Surfing California,* by Bank Wright. An older guide to the best surfing beaches, written in inimitable surf-speak by one of the legends.

- *Surfing San Onofre to Point Dume, 1936–1942,* by Don James.

- *Surfing: The Sport of Hawaiian Kings,* by Ben R. Finney and James D. Houston.

- *Surfing: The Ultimate Pleasure,* by Leonard Lucernos. By general consensus, this is the best history of the sport.

- *The Big Drop! Classic Big Wave Surfing Stories,* by John Long and Hai Van Sponholz (eds.).

- *The Encyclopedia of Surfing,* by Matt Warshaw. Includes 1,500 entries on surfing, arranged encyclopedia-style by a noted surf writer who has authored three other books on the sport.

- *The Surfin'ary,* by Trevor Cralle. There are 3,000 entries in this surfer's dictionary.

- *Waikiki Beach Boys,* by Grady Timmons. A chronicle of the original Hawaiians who gave the world the sport of surfing.

The **California Surf Museum** (223 North Coast Highway, Oceanside, 760/721-6876) is a good place to begin your hunt for many of these titles. Some are out of print, but you might luck out at used bookstores and eBay!

being situated at the foot of a hill blocks from the Pacific. A generic trailer park bears the misleadingly pastoral name Mobile Village—Valley of Dreams.

Still, folks in Leucadia live and let live, work construction jobs when available, eat tacos and brown rice, use environmentally safe products, and stare unconcerned when cars pass through town. They simply don't need vacationers in Leucadia, which is just as well, because the beaches aren't big enough to attract them and the cliffs are eroding. The sign at one washed-out beach access had this spray-painted addendum: No tourists. Go home. It might as well have read: No beach. Go home. In a funny way, being so removed from the breakneck world of the 21st century, it's the sort of place we don't just like visiting but could see ourselves calling home.

For more information, contact the Encinitas Chamber of Commerce, 859 Second Street, Encinitas, CA 92024, 760/753-6041, www.encinitaschamber.com; or the San Diego North Convention & Visitors Bureau, 360 North Escondido Boulevard, Escondido, CA 92025, 760/745-4741 or 800/848-3336, www.sandiegonorth.com.

BEACHES

The beaches of Encinitas generally look a lot healthier in this decade than they did the previous one, thanks to a major sand renourishment project. Still, you can renourish the beaches all you want, but you're only buying time and wasting money. A wise investor would not want to own oceanfront property in Encinitas, no matter how splendid the view. Signs warn, Unstable Cliffs and Frequent Bluff Failure, and the sandstone along this stretch of coast is especially prone to erosion. At least in the short term, the beaches of Encinitas are more fun to play on than they've been in a while.

Starting from the south, **Swami's Surf Beach** is below Seacliff Roadside Park (free parking, day-use only), a bluff-top city park at the south end of the Self-Realization Fellowship Retreat, Gardens, and Hermitage.

During the winter, this is surfer heaven, and in the summer it still offers plenty of rough fun for surf riders. A long stairwell topped by white wooden crests leads along the cliff face to a fabled small beach. Surfers bob a good distance from shore while lifeguards look on. The cliff face has been reinforced with plantings, and the stretch of bluff from here north to D Street has been designated a Marine Life Refuge. Swami's Cafe is across from the Moonie temple and the beach.

Just above Swami's, and accessible only on foot, is **Boneyard Beach.** At low tide, small, protective coves afford romantics, nudists, and surfers privacy for their various activities. Just don't get caught by a rising tide with your drawers down.

D Street Viewpoint is accessible at the end of D Street in Encinitas. Steps lead down to a rock-backed city-run beach not unlike Swami's, with a lifeguard. Speaking of views, we caught a dandy one at the D Street beach overlook. Stairs descend along the cliff face, with gorgeous plantings on either side. At the top of the stairs, we admired both the beach vista and a nearly perfect specimen of California pulchritude hanging out with her surfer pals. This is, we decided, what is meant by California dreaming.

At the foot of Encinitas Boulevard is **Moonlight Beach,** the centerpiece of the coast in these parts. There's a free municipal parking lot, plenty of facilities, volleyball nets, pumped-in sand, and a pack of happy sunbathers. If you're not partaking of the party on the sand—and Moonlight Beach is one of the most accessible and popular beaches in north San Diego County—then you should at least drop by to gaze down on the action from the bluff-top parking lot. What a view! Just one troubling thing: Water quality has historically been a cloudy issue at Moonlight Beach, owing to its proximity to a sewage treatment plant.

The access to **Stone Steps Beach** is on Neptune Avenue. Park for free in the quiet neighborhood along Neptune's curbs and climb down the steep and plentiful (97 by our count) stone steps, paying homage to the mural of a mermaid on the half-shell. A lifeguard stand, marked with surf and tide advisories, is at the bottom of the stairwell. The beach attracts scores of surfers. If you walk north from Stone Steps Beach, you'll reach the **Encinitas Beach.** There is no other direct access to it from shore, which makes it secluded enough to please space-seeking swimmers, surfers, and solitary sorts.

Formerly Leucadia State Beach but now a city-managed area, **Beacon's Beach** lies at the foot of a yellow sandstone cliff and can be reached by hiking down a treacherous trail of sandbags, stairs, and switchbacks. You can park for free at the Beacon's Beach access and scuttle down to the beach, where the copious kelp that washes ashore gets entangled with the equally abundant litter. You can look up and down the coast from the base of the cliffs at Beacon's Beach and see the same things: steep, eroding cliffs and packs of surfers competing for waves. From "Kenzie of Leucadia," a Beacon's booster: "Locals love to boast that the only place more crowded than our line-up is I-5 at rush hour after a heavy rainstorm."

Above the beach in the lot, a roving surfing instructor (his van read "Kahuna Bob's Surf School") was giving preliminary lessons to a group of youngsters who looked so eager to hit the water that they were positively shivering with excitement. (Call **Kahuna Bob's Surf School,** 760/721-7700.) Beyond them, another Leucadia resident, also a surfer, stared wistfully at Beacon's rugged waves. He'd suffered a shoulder injury in a nasty spill some weeks earlier and found himself beached until it healed. In the meantime he pedaled a bike to stay in shape, but it just wasn't the same. Leucadia was his alternative to Pacific Beach, where he'd been living until he was squeezed out by mounting crowds and rents. Pacific Beach had, in turn, been his alternative to Ocean Beach, which had been his alternative to Imperial Beach. Gradually, he said, he will make his way north to the magic land of Santa Barbara. "I want to live

at the beach forever," he announced with no solicitation. For now Leucadia is home; relaxed, uncrowded, and nontrendy, it is his isle of paradise. Besides, he knows someone with private access to the beach.

At the north end of Neptune Avenue is **Grandview,** another city-run beach access. It's nicely landscaped, with palm trees running down the hill beside the stairwell. It's a grand spot from which to wistfully gaze at the horizon, especially at sunset.

SWAMI'S SURF BEACH

Location: 1298 First Street, below Seacliff Roadside Park in Encinitas
Parking/Fees: free parking lot
Hours: 5 A.M.-10 P.M.
Facilities: lifeguards, restrooms, and picnic area
Contact: Encinitas Parks and Recreation, 760/633-2740

BONEYARD BEACH

Location: in Encinitas north of Swami's, between E and J Streets
Parking/Fees: free street parking
Hours: 5 A.M.-10 P.M.
Facilities: none
Contact: Encinitas Parks and Recreation, 760/633-2740

D STREET VIEWPOINT

Location: in Encinitas at 450 D Street
Parking/Fees: free parking lot
Hours: 5 A.M.-10 P.M.
Facilities: lifeguards
Contact: Encinitas Parks and Recreation, 760/633-2740

Swami's Surf Beach

38 MOONLIGHT BEACH

Location: in Encinitas at Fourth and B Streets
Parking/Fees: free parking lot
Hours: 5 A.M.-10 P.M.
Facilities: lifeguards, restrooms, showers, picnic tables, and fire rings
Contact: Encinitas Parks and Recreation, 760/633-2740

39 STONE STEPS BEACH

Location: in Encinitas at Neptune Avenue and El Portal Street
Parking/Fees: free street parking
Hours: 5 A.M.-10 P.M.
Facilities: lifeguards
Contact: Encinitas Parks and Recreation, 760/633-2740

40 ENCINITAS BEACH

Location: in Encinitas north of Stone Steps Beach
Parking/Fees: free street parking at Stone Steps Beach
Hours: 5 A.M.-10 P.M.
Facilities: none
Contact: Encinitas Parks and Recreation, 760/633-2740

41 BEACON'S BEACH

Location: in Leucadia at 948 Neptune Avenue
Parking/Fees: free street parking
Hours: 5 A.M.-10 P.M.
Facilities: lifeguards
Contact: Encinitas Parks and Recreation, 760/633-2740

42 GRANDVIEW

Location: in Leucadia at the north end of Neptune Avenue
Parking/Fees: free parking lot
Hours: 5 A.M.–10 P.M.
Facilities: none
Contact: Encinitas Parks and Recreation, 760/633-2740

RECREATION AND ATTRACTIONS

- **Bike/Skate Rentals:** B & L Bike, 211 North Coast Highway, Solana Beach, 858/481-4148; Nytro, 940 South Coast Highway, Encinitas, 800/697-8007

- **Ecotourism:** San Elijo Lagoon Ecological Reserve, Cardiff-by-the-Sea, 760/436-3944

- **Rainy Day Attraction:** Self-Realization Fellowship Retreat, Gardens, and Hermitage, 215 K Street, Encinitas, 760/753-2888

- **Shopping/Browsing:** Carlsbad Company Stores, Paseo del Norte, Carlsbad, 760/804-9000

- **Surf Shop:** Solana Beach Surf Shop, 363 U.S. 101, Solana Beach, 760/481-1354; Salty Sister, 2796 Carlsbad Boulevard, Carlsbad, 760/434-1122

- **Vacation Rentals:** A&N, 6986 El Camino Real, Suite H, Carlsbad, 760/438-6811

ACCOMMODATIONS

Beware of motels with "Ocean" or "Beach" in their names that are located on a highway bypass nowhere near a beach. In particular they should be avoided in Encinitas and Leucadia, where flyblown motels tout "sea breezes" and "views" when the only views they offer are of traffic and consignment shops. The only place that's actually on the beach in either town is the **Moonlight Beach Motel** (233 Second Street, 760/753-0623, $), a functional and affordable three-story place with balcony views of the town's biggest beach.

The **Pacific Surf Inn** (1076 North U.S. 101, 760/436-8763, $) in Leucadia has a clean, well-tended appearance. An offbeat alternative is **Leucadia Inn-by-the-Sea** (960 North Coast Highway, Leucadia, 760/942-1668, $$). Though it's not "by" the sea but three blocks away on a busy highway, its six "whimsical theme rooms" will amuse lovers of roadside oddities. They range from African Safari to Hollywood Nostalgia, and from Nantucket to Mexico, which is quite a geographic spread.

Other viable bunking options are the campground at San Elijo State Beach, straddling Cardiff-by-the-Sea and Encinitas, and a **Holiday Inn Express** (607 Leucadia Boulevard, 760/944-3800, $) in Leucadia.

COASTAL CUISINE

Along U.S. 101 to the south, Encinitas is top-heavy with Italian and Mexican cafés. Their shopping-plaza backdrops are good indicators of the predictable fare they offer. Keep driving up the road to **DB Hackers** (101 Old U.S. 101, 760/436-3162, $), which serves good, quick fixes of seafood. The entrées are mostly fried and the outdoor patio treats you to car noise and construction, but the staff is friendly and the food is relatively cheap. We were more than sufficiently rejuvenated by the fish tacos we ate and the Jimmy Cliff tunes that were playing.

For breakfast head to **George's Restaurant** (641 South U.S. 101, 760/942-9549, $), a legendary hangout that was the original home of the California Surf Museum (now in Oceanside). The specialty is Surf's Up, a no-nonsense protein-heavy feed with scrambled eggs, ham, and American cheese on an English muffin, served with hash browns.

NIGHTLIFE

The friendliest bar in town is the **Full Moon Saloon** (485 First Street, 760/436-7397), which offers live music and a game room. More live music can be found at **First Street Bar** (656 First Street, 760/944-0233), which is popular with locals and is regularly voted best neighborhood bar.

Encinitas and Leucadia have, over the years, attracted a sizable contingent of New Age groupies and ex-hippies, some of whom can be found knocking back soy-milk lattes at the **Naked Bean Coffee Co.** (1126 First Street, 760/634-1347). The Naked Bean also features live music on weekends.

Carlsbad

Carlsbad is an anomaly. Of all the towns that cling to the Southern California coast, it is the only one not founded by a Spaniard or profoundly shaped by Latin influences. Instead, Carlsbad was the brainstorm of Gerhard Schutte, a German who came west from Nebraska to found a town of "small farms and gracious homes." His dream was made possible in 1883, when the Arizona Eastern Railway was completed, linking Southern California with the rest of civilization. This line also opened the land between Los Angeles and San Diego to homesteaders. Schutte headed up the list and moved on out.

Spanish and Native American influences are not entirely absent from the historical record. For centuries prior to Schutte's arrival, the Luseino tribe lived on the land between the two lagoons that form the boundaries of Carlsbad. However, they were quickly run off or subjugated by the missions when, in 1769, conquistador Gaspar de Portolá arrived with his faith-filled sidekick, Father Juan Crespi. Even though the entire area was under Spanish rule, the only lingering trace of their influence today is Agua Hedionda, the name given to one of the local lagoons. It means "stinking waters."

By the time Schutte arrived, the mission system was destroyed and the land grab was on. Schutte and his followers purchased a chunk of real estate and began planting eucalyptus trees and squaring off lots for a town. In the process they discovered that the mineral water from their wells was identical to that found at the renowned Ninth Spa in Karlsbad, Bohemia (now Karlovy Vary, in the Czech Republic).

The town took its name and identity from that happenstance, becoming a bastion of Old Europe in the New World. When word got out about the water, settlers began arriving. Humble, hardworking, and mostly English, these folks built their town to reflect their no-nonsense values.

Surprisingly little of the town has changed to this day. Original buildings are restored, and the subsequent growth of the town adheres to an established code, allowing Carlsbad to call itself a "village by the sea" (albeit a very high-toned and expensive village). With its Victorian, Dutch, and Bohemian architecture, Carlsbad has retained an appealingly antiquarian personality. This is remarkable, considering that Carlsbad lies between the drab military metropolis of Oceanside and the teeming asphalt sprawl of metropolitan San Diego.

Some of the local buildings—such as Magee House, Twin Inns, and the Santa Fe Railway Station—have been designated National Historic Landmarks. The best place to orient yourself to town history is the Visitor Information Center, inside the **Santa Fe Railway Station** on Carlsbad Village Drive. Built in 1887, it's the oldest commercial structure in town.

Another must-see is the **Alt Karlsbad Haus,** on Carlsbad Boulevard. Built in 1964 on the site of the first mineral well, it's an exact replica of Antonín Dvořák's house in Prague. The great composer, whose patriotic *New World Symphony* had achieved national notoriety when the town was founded, is honored by a plaque on one wall. On another wall is a plaque that reads, "The formation of the Hanseatic League in the 13th century gave birth to modern civilization, and through commerce and trade lifted Europe out of the Dark Ages." This is not the sort of plaque one is accustomed to reading in Southern California. Incidentally, Dvořák was a Bohemian who, out of love for his adopted home, offered to write a new national anthem for America. His spirit is a fitting one to symbolize the village of Carlsbad, which has lifted itself above

ALL ABOARD THE COASTER!

The Coaster is a "beach train" that offers regular rail service at eight stops in San Diego, Solana Beach, Encinitas, Carlsbad, and Oceanside. The Coaster also serves Old Town and downtown San Diego and Sorrento Valley. Environmentally, it is a viable alternative, burning low-sulfur-content fuel with high efficiency, greatly reducing particulate emissions. When operating at full capacity, each Coaster car means 700 fewer cars from I-5.

The Coaster carried 700,000 passengers during 1995, its first year of operation. By 2004, it was carrying 1.4 million passengers annually. The train is also good for one's mental health, sparing you the stress of highway car travel. The Coaster is scenic, too, running on tracks that parallel the ocean for most of its route. It operates from early morning to early evening, Monday through Saturday. At each station, you are dropped off a few short paces from the beach. Northern San Diego County has also instituted **The Breeze,** a clean-running bus system, and **The Sprinter,** which uses the first Diesel Multiple Units in the country to propel light rail trains.

For more information, contact **North County Transit District,** 810 Mission Avenue, Oceanside, CA 92054, 760/966-6500, www.gonctd.com.

the Dark Ages of the early 21st century by holding fast to civilized values.

Today, Carlsbad (population 95,500) seems to have everything going for it. Its public school system is one of the best in the country. The unemployment rate is the lowest in San Diego County. The public library is larger than some college libraries. The average daily temperature ranges from 58 degrees in January to 73 degrees in July. The young people look healthy, happy, well-groomed, and tattoo-free. ("Hey, John," one Beaver Cleaver look-alike yelled out a car window to a pal, "your new haircut looks great!") The old folks who choose to live out their years here look contented, too. After a few hours, you begin to wonder if this isn't the town Norman Rockwell was painting all those years.

Yes, Carlsbad is not just a place to vacation. It's a place to settle down and attend the church of your choice. This is a town of churches: Lutheran rest homes stand hard by humble Hispanic Pentecostal churches. We passed one of the latter, a sort of Quonset hut with a steeple, on the way to dinner. The door was open to the street and we heard the congregation singing and banging drums and tambourines. Two hours later, on our return

stroll, they were still at it, exhorted by a shouting minister.

Of the 37 square miles that fall within the city limits, less than one half have been developed, and the residents are vigilant against creeping mall sprawl. According to a resident, "We're putting the screws on too much more growth." Of course there's always something nipping at those Utopian heels. Most recently, it's a children's theme park called Legoland ("your destination for real family fun!"), which was built on Carlsbad Ranch, east of town. California's first new theme park in 25 years, the 128-acre **Legoland California** (1 Lego Drive, 760/918-5346) opened in March 1999 with much fanfare. Legoland has nine play areas inside the park, including Explore Village, Dino Town, Fun Town, and Land of Adventure. There are more than 50 rides on property. World landmarks, animals, and what-have-you have been rendered in plastic Lego bricks by the millions. There's also a Sea Life U.S. aquarium, a recent addition, which costs extra.

We don't know what it all signifies, but this much we can tell you: Adults pay $60 per day ($75 for a two-day pass), while kids 16 and under and seniors 61 and over are charged $50 apiece ($65 for a two-day pass). In addition, you're hit with a $10 parking fee. A family of four will spend $230 for a day at Legoland California even before the kids whine for their first soda pop or souvenir trinket.

We're more inclined to head to **Carlsbad Mineral Water Spa** (2802 Carlsbad Boulevard, 760/434-1887) for a rejuvenating soak. It's been around since 1882 and is a California Historic Site. More to the point, the pure water that comes from a 1,700-foot aquifer is 9,500 years old and full of rejuvenating minerals. The spa offers body wraps, massages, mud facials, mineral baths, and more.

For more information, contact the Carlsbad Convention and Visitors Bureau, 400 Carlsbad Village Drive, Carlsbad, CA 92008, 760/434-6093 or 800/227-5722, www.visit carlsbad.com; the Carlsbad Chamber of Commerce, 5934 Priestly Drive, Carlsbad, CA 92008, 760/931-8400, www.carlsbad.org; or San Diego North Convention & Visitors Bureau, 360 North Escondido Boulevard, Escondido, CA 92025, 760/745-4741 or 800/848-3336, www.sandiegonorth.com.

BEACHES

A good deal of the beach in the Carlsbad area eroded since the construction of Oceanside Harbor to the north, and El Niño storms claimed more of the sand in the late 1990s. You never know what you'll find in any given year on the beaches of Carlsbad: a sandless, eroded plain of cobbles or a newly renourished beach that hasn't yet washed away.

Coming from the south, **Ponto Beach**—a unit of South Carlsbad State Beach—is up first. It's by Batiquitos Lagoon, between Carlsbad and Leucadia. The location is a bit distressed, with an ad hoc string of parking spaces along the west side of Carlsbad Boulevard (U.S. 101). A rusty chain-link fence keeps people away from the crumbling cliff edges. There's an abandoned parking lot and fences everywhere. The future is not promising, and the present at Ponto is fairly dismal. Though surfers still get their kicks here, it's not the kind of place others would go out of their way to visit.

The main unit of **South Carlsbad State Beach** is in some disarray, too. At one time, this was a highly desirable 226-site state-park campground occupying an inspirational bluff-top setting overlooking the beach. Now campers are shoehorned into a narrow strip between the eroding cliffs and the four-lane boulevard. South Carlsbad appears to be fighting a losing battle against the elements. In some forthcoming year, the campground will succumb and the road will be next. Already, you can see stretches of U.S. 101 (designated "Old Coast Road") that have been abandoned and relocated east.

South Carlsbad State Beach runs into **Carlsbad State Beach,** which runs for four miles. A portion of Carlsbad State Beach has been designated **Tamarack Surf Beach** (where Tamarack Avenue meets Carlsbad Boulevard). This is a busy place; we found the sizable parking lot at Tamarack full on a Monday afternoon around sunset. Carlsbad State Beach is popular with all sorts of recreating types: bodysurfers, boogie boarders, swimmers, divers, and surf casters. Incidentally, another in-town stretch of sand has been designated **Robert C. Frazee State Beach,** but it (like Tamarack Surf Beach) is part of Carlsbad State Beach. The city of Carlsbad is none too happy that the state of California has decided to charge $8 per car to park at formerly free Tamarack. In fact the city has sued the California Coastal Commission to prohibit the charge, and the case was going to court as we were going to press. (Speaking of lawsuits, in 2007 the city of Carlsbad agreed to pay $12.5 million to residents of a condo complex after a landslide, caused by city-pipe discharges, destroyed eight condos.)

Carlsbad is a great town for walking, especially along its beaches. Two jogging/biking paths—one that runs beside Carlsbad Boulevard and one below it by the seawall that protects the beach—draw a tireless troupe of

California aerobicizers. They jog, they bike, they racewalk, they skateboard, they huff and puff…anything to maintain those hourglass figures. We watched a pair of toned-up girls sprinting up and down the stairs that link Carlsbad's pathways while conversing breathlessly about clothes, dates, and office politics. Many bring along their dogs, who run with their owners or pull them on skateboards.

The north part of town has been generously seeded with street-end accesses, each of which has stairs that lead to the beach (but no facilities). As in south Oceanside, north Carlsbad is a largely middle-class residential neighborhood, and the main point of these accesses appears to be to allow local residents to get to the beach.

Believe it or not, the "stinking waters" at **Agua Hedionda Lagoon** (east of Carlsbad City Beach) are popular with swimmers and water-skiers. Boats and water-skis can be rented at **Snug Harbor Marina** (4215 Harrison Street, 760/434-3089). A nice hiking/biking trail runs along the shore of the lagoon.

43 PONTO BEACH

Location: between Leucadia and Carlsbad on Old U.S. 101. Take the La Costa Drive exit off I-5 and follow it until it ends at Old U.S. 101 (Carlsbad Avenue) at Batiquitos Lagoon.
Parking/Fees: free roadside parking
Hours: dawn-sunset
Facilities: restrooms, showers, picnic tables, and barbecue grills
Contact: South Carlsbad State Beach, 760/438-3143

44 SOUTH CARLSBAD STATE BEACH

Location: three miles south of Carlsbad, along Carlsbad Boulevard

Parking/Fees: $8 entrance fee per vehicle; camping fees $20-25 per night inland, $30-35 per night beachfront, plus $7.50 reservation fee
Hours: dawn-sunset
Facilities: lifeguards, restrooms, showers, and picnic tables.
Contact: South Carlsbad State Beach, 760/438-3143

45 TAMARACK SURF BEACH

Location: Carlsbad Boulevard at Tamarack Avenue in Carlsbad
Parking/Fees: $8 entrance fee per vehicle
Hours: dawn-sunset
Facilities: lifeguards, restrooms, and picnic tables
Contact: South Carlsbad State Beach, 760/438-3143

46 ROBERT C. FRAZEE STATE BEACH

Location: in Carlsbad along Carlsbad Boulevard at Ocean Street
Parking/Fees: free street parking
Hours: dawn-sunset
Facilities: none
Contact: South Carlsbad State Beach, 760/438-3143

ACCOMMODATIONS

It's not cheap to stay in the "village by the sea." The village mentality can be a little tough on the wallet. **La Costa Resort & Spa** (2100 Costa del Mar Road, 760/438-9111, www.la costa.com, $$$$), a 500-room golf and tennis resort, attracts celebrities by the Lear-jet load and hosts golf and tennis tournaments. It's got two PGA courses and 21 tennis courts, plus a spa and "Chopra Center" (as in Deepak, the New Age guru), where you can "harness your creative genius, create perfect health, and access blissful, peaceful states of existence." With room rates that range $340–520 nightly (more for suites), you'll need all the bliss you can lay your hands on.

A few steps down in price and many steps closer to the beach is the **Carlsbad Inn Beach Resort** (3075 Carlsbad Boulevard, 760/434-7020 or 800/235-3939, www.carlsbadinn.com, $$$), an appealing beach and tennis complex built in the center of town under the community's watchful Old World architectural guidelines. A swimming pool, workout room, and kids' spa make this a winner. Another worthy beachfront choice is the **Tamarack Beach Resort** (3200 Carlsbad Boulevard, 760/729-3500, www.tamarackresort.com, $$$), which is more like a time-share condominium than a motel. Each suite has a washer and dryer, full kitchen, and stereo.

For a front and center location on the beach, you can't better the **Best Western Beach Terrace Inn** (2775 Ocean Street, 760/729-5951, www.beachterraceinn.com, $$$). Located in a quiet residential neighborhood, the Beach Terrace Inn has as sunny a disposition as you'll find at the beach. Plus, you can practically jump off the balcony into the ocean (though we'd advise against it). Nearly as appealing is the **Best Western Beach View Lodge** (3180 Carlsbad Boulevard, 760/729-1151, $$), which lies close to but not quite on the ocean and will earn you a significant break on rates relative to the other resorts and inns mentioned herein.

COASTAL CUISINE

If you like fried seafood, it can be ordered by the basket at **Harbor Fish South** (3179 Carlsbad Boulevard, 760/729-4161, $), an outdoor-patio joint beside the ocean and next to a surf shop. The clientele is young and not very discriminating about their diet. The Surfer's Special, for instance, is a cheeseburger and fries. But the view and ambience are perfectly beachy. Somewhat disappointingly, the fish in the fish 'n' chips basket is not local but comes from Alaskan waters.

The best local seafood we found was at **Fish House Vera Cruz** (417 Carlsbad Village Drive, 760/434-6777, $$), a pleasant stroll over the railroad tracks just east of the town center. The name derives from a fishing boat that scours the Pacific coast from Baja to Alaska to nab the goodies they serve here. Everything is mesquite-grilled to perfection, and prices are moderate. The place even looks like the hold of a fishing vessel, with lots of nautical knickknacks.

Niemans (300 Carlsbad Village Drive, 760/729-4131, $$$) is worth visiting because it's housed in the oldest Victorian structure in town. If you're not inclined toward "proper attire," you can at least stroll the grounds and pretend to be studying the menu, which tends toward hearty fare (prime rib, filet mignon, leg of lamb) with a smattering of seafood items.

NIGHTLIFE

In a Norman Rockwell kind of town, you're lucky to find a place that serves even something as harmless as frozen yogurt after dark. Carlsbad, fortunately, does have a semblance of nightlife. The primary source of activity is **Sandbar Cafe** (3878 Carlsbad Boulevard, 760/729-3170), which sits across the street from the roaring ocean surf and is home to live rock and blues on many nights. Another hopping haunt is the local **Hennessey's Tavern** (2777 Roosevelt Street, 760/729-6951), which has live music on weekends. For more low-key good times, the **Kafana Coffee Shop** (3076 Carlsbad Boulevard, 760/720-0074) offers warbling folkies and good, stiff belts of caffeine.

Oceanside

For decades Oceanside has been a sprawling military/urban wasteland. Though the reputation hasn't changed much over the years, the city lately appears to be on the upswing. Yes, the past is behind Oceanside and the future's so bright you gotta wear shades. At least it's been sprucing itself up and putting its best foot forward, and we're pleased to report that Oceanside has been steadily improving since we first began visiting in the mid-1980s. Back then, it wore the sad-sack look of a military town that existed largely to serve the practical and prurient needs of thousands of U.S. Marines stationed at Camp Pendleton. Although we certainly wouldn't describe it as a destination mecca for those traveling the California coast, there's no reason to actively avoid it these days, either.

To fully understand Oceanside (population 170,000), it's necessary to do like the Marines and hit the beaches. You would expect a town with a name like Oceanside to be blessed in that department. From Buccaneer Beach to Oceanside Pier to Harbor Beach, this unpretentious place has been adopted by beachgoers from as far afield as Encinitas. They come to Oceanside because their own beaches are either crowded or disappearing, and because parking is easier, prices are cheaper, and attitudes are conducive to casual enjoyment.

Even given these enviable conditions, Oceanside has a tale of woe regarding the beach that sits on either side of the formidable Oceanside Pier (which, at 1,942 feet, is the second longest on the West Coast). According to the still-angry locals, the main culprit is the U.S. Army Corps of Engineers. In the 1960s, having conducted only minimal study of the impact on the surrounding coastline, the Corps created a harbor at Oceanside. This one is big, slick, and modern, with 950 slips for pleasure craft and yachts, a marina, restaurants, condominiums, and a shopping plaza designed to resemble a Cape Cod seaport village.

Before the architectural surgery, Oceanside had one of the widest, longest, and best-loved beaches on the southern coast. It was a Sahara of sand that was especially attractive to surfers. Imagine, if you will, a sea monster coming ashore and taking a five-acre bite out of the center of this beach, then spitting the sand back into the water several miles offshore.

This, essentially, is what has happened in Oceanside. According to a local historian who was in high school at the time, he and his classmates, as a science project, conducted a study of the proposed harbor project. They foresaw the damage that would be done to their beloved beach. They presented their study to the Corps and were basically told, "Beat it, kids, you don't know what you're t alking about."

Alas, they did know. Photographs of Oceanside City Beach taken in 1946 show an uninterrupted swath of sand as wide and straight as any we've seen on either coast. The same beach today is certainly lovely to behold, but it's nowhere near the size of the beach back in the 1940s. The jetty that was meant to ward off rough waters from luxury vessels in the harbor was built at the wrong angle. The sand that normally flowed south with the longshore currents in years past now winds up at the bottom of an offshore canyon, lost forever. To make this tale even more shameful, the Army Corps of Engineers must dredge the harbor two or three times a year to keep it navigable. "It's amazing that Carlsbad doesn't sue the Corps," opined our local historian, referring to the devastating effects of the disrupted sand flow south of Oceanside. "It's a pretty big thing to lose your beach."

Thankfully, a sand-bypassing operation has been developed that has begun to replenish the shoreline. It involves shooting sand through six-inch tubes located around the harbor, where it can resume its natural southerly drift with the currents. In a sense, Oceanside has lost and found its beach. And it has been gearing up for bigger things. The 100 acres behind the pier—except for the California Surf Museum—have been slated for development. The Marriott hotel chain has already signed on, and four 10-story buildings are on the drawing board. But unlike the residents of most coastal towns, the natives aren't opposed to a massive facelift in Oceanside. We'd agree that, for once, it actually makes sense.

CALIFORNIA SURF MUSEUM

As everyone knows, surfing is more than a sport. In Southern California, perhaps more than anywhere else except Hawaii, it is a religion. Around these parts, the church of choice is the California Surf Museum, near the Oceanside Pier.

The museum's history is not unlike that of a wandering religious mystic. Founded in 1985 by Jane Schmauss and Stuart Resor, it was originally housed at George's Restaurant in Encinitas. It moved to Pacific Beach, then back to Encinitas's Moonlight Plaza. Finally it arrived at its Canaan — a former VFW hall and beach bar in the heart of surfer country.

The California Surf Museum is a delight for devotees of the sport and the merely curious. The history and lore of surfing are lovingly told with original relics, informative placards, vintage photographs, clothing, clippings, books, and shrines to dead surfers. Exhibits are changed regularly, and various events celebrate the sport's history, which is particularly rich in this locale. The most sacred moments and mementos are devoted to the pantheon of greats who've taken that one last ride to surfer heaven. Their stories read like the lives of saints. They include:

- George Freeth, the Hawaiian who introduced surfing to California and then became a lifeguard in Oceanside. Freeth died of pneumonia in 1910 after rescuing several people in the rough waters off Oceanside Pier.

- Leroy "Granny" Grannis and Doc Ball, two great surfers who were also the first surf photographers. They understood that no one can take pictures of surfers in action better than those who understand the sport from the inside.

- Duke Kahanamoku, the Polynesian who popularized surfing worldwide. He also reintroduced surfing to Hawaii after missionaries had forbidden it. He took his nickname from the Duke of Edinburgh and won three gold medals in swimming at the 1912 Olympics. One of the Duke's redwood longboards is on display at the museum.

- Bob Simmons, a daredevil whose only possessions were a 1937 Ford and a longboard. He developed the "spoon nose" (a lift at the front of the board that helps avoid nosedives) and was the first surfer to use rope hand grips. He was inexhaustible, surfing from sunup to sundown. On September 27, 1954, while surfing Windansea in La Jolla, Simmons caught a bigger wave than even he could handle. His board made it to shore, but he never did.

Anecdotes like these and the countless items for perusal and sale bring surfing alive, even for the uninitiated.

For more information, contact the California Surf Museum (223 North Coast Highway, Oceanside, CA 92054, 760/721-6876, www.surfmuseum.org). The museum is open daily from 10 A.M.-4 P.M. Admission is free, though donations are welcome.

"It won't be Cement City, like they did to Huntington Beach," a longtime local told us. "It will be more like a seaport village, made of wood, with an educational Sea Center. We want it." After all it's been through, the rough-and-tumble city of Oceanside deserves whatever upscaling it can wrangle.

The main reason for Oceanside's size and almost the sole reason for its existence is **Camp Pendleton.** Occupying 250,000 acres (200 square miles), it is the world's largest U.S. Marine base. Camp Pendleton is literally next door to Oceanside, its back gate opening onto Oceanside Harbor. Sixty thousand marine and civilian personnel work and train at the camp. Those who don't live on base reside in Oceanside with their families.

At first glimpse Oceanside doesn't look like the stereotypical military town. Great pains have been made to disguise this fact, especially on the water. Still, Oceanside is at its core a military town, and this makes for such incongruities as a champagne brunch at the Taste of Europe restaurant two blocks from the Paradise-by-the-Sea RV Park. It may not be a bona fide war zone, as many landlocked military towns are. But as you pull away from the upscale harbor you begin to notice more liquor stores than you might expect to see in a town of this size. Broken-bulb saloons, low-rent food stands, thrift shops, discount clothiers, and flat-roofed duplexes—all are signs of a military lifestyle that has remained largely unchanged since World War II. No slight intended, as one of us was an army brat who spent the happiest years of his childhood on and around military bases.

Incidentally, the **Buena Vista Lagoon Ecological Reserve** is south of town, between Oceanside and Carlsbad. This large natural wetland—one of the few remaining in Southern California—is a habitat for birds and vegetation (including rare species of both). A trail along the shoreline makes for pleasant sightings. The **Buena Vista Audubon Nature Center** (2202 South Coast Highway, 760/439-2473) provides exhibits, lectures, and group tours; it's open 10 A.M.–2 P.M. Tuesday–Saturday.

Oh yes, extra credit is available for those willing to drive four miles inland on Highway 76 to see **Mission San Luis Rey de Francia** (4050 Mission Avenue, 760/757-3651). Founded in 1798 by Father Fermin de Lasuen, the "King of the Missions" was named for King Louis XI of France. The largest of the Franciscan-run missions, it was lavishly decorated to be something of a showpiece. Today, it houses an active order of Franciscan monks and a museum, which is open to the public for viewing and souvenir buying. A fiesta is held here every year during the third week of July. Of particular interest are the paintings by local Native Americans.

For more information, contact the Oceanside Chamber of Commerce, 928 North Coast Highway, Oceanside, CA 92054, 760/722-1534, www.oceansidechamber.com; or San Diego North Convention & Visitors Bureau, 360 N. Escondido Boulevard, Escondido, CA 92025, 760/745-4741 or 800/848-3336, www.sandiegonorth.com.

BEACHES

Palm-lined Pacific Street runs along Oceanside's beach from the south end of town up to Oceanside Pier. Hereabouts is a pleasant residential neighborhood of newish homes that betray a fondness for the New England architectural style rather than the Spanish vernacular of stucco and pipe roofs one generally finds in Southern California. Beach accesses are plentiful at street ends and parking on side streets is abundant. At the south end, however, a wall of riprap boulders protects homes from the ocean's incursions along a section of shoreline.

Oceanside's sandy bounty begins inauspiciously with **South Oceanside Beach** (on South Pacific Street). You park in the neighborhood along an enormous cement embankment and pass between condos onto hard-packed sand; not worth the trouble, as much better beaches lie ahead.

More easily accessed is **Buccaneer Beach,** which is in the same residential neighborhood.

The beach here is a tiny pocket of sand free of rocks and debris. It's nice, but nicer still is pondering what the beach would be like if it weren't hogged by all the houses built right on top of it. Across the street is **Buccaneer Park,** an inviting green space with play area, picnic tables, snack bar, restrooms, and showers. Also quite nice is **Loma Alta Marsh,** a small lagoon east of the beach. A trail passes beneath a railroad trestle, and birds can be heard chirping happily.

Several more beach accesses with lifeguard towers are strewn between Buccaneer Park and Oceanside Pier. Named for the streets that meet Pacific Street in their vicinity, they are (from south to north) **Oceanside Boulevard Beach, Wisconsin Street Beach,** and **Tyson Street Beach.** The last of these has a park with picnic tables and playground, much as at Buccaneer Park. It's hard not to like Oceanside from the perspective of these grassy seaside parks and broad, sandy beaches.

A one-way oceanfront street with benches and green space called The Strand flares off of Pacific Street south of the pier and rejoins it just north of the pier. It's great for family strolls or lonely naps in the grass. Down by **Oceanside Pier,** you'll find a wide, pleasant beach extending in both directions. A sand renourishment project undertaken in 2001 has for the most part remained in place along this popular stretch. (Of course, all that could change in a single stormy winter.) The area south of the pier is called **Pier View South.** It is a narrower strand than the beach between the pier and breakwater, which is designated **Pier View North.**

The beach just south of Oceanside Harbor is called **Breakwater Way,** and it is a quiet, safe, and relatively out-of-the-way family beach. The jetties up at this end of Oceanside protect the mouth of the San Luis Rey River. North of the river is Oceanside Harbor and **Harbor Beach.** Because it abuts the north jetty, which intercepts the ocean's attempted transport of sand across the river mouth, Harbor Beach is among the widest beaches in San Diego County. The beach and harbor area are filled with amenities, from picnic tables and volleyball nets to deep-sea fishing trips and kayak rentals. Motels, shops, and restaurants, too! Oceanside Harbor even has its own fishing pier, making this a two-pier town.

The beaches in the vicinity of the pier can get crowded on summer weekends, but owing to the fact that Oceanside is a military town and not a tourist destination—or even a huge favorite with day-tripping inlanders—it is not as jammed as other in-town beaches in northern San Diego County (which is one more reason to come here). The Oceanside town planners have done their best to make the pier an inviting area, with stands of palm trees, green and cleanly kept park space, a pierside amphitheater, and concessions (including, unfortunately, a McDonald's, which says volumes about the typical beach visitor). The sand is soft, light brown, and well patrolled by lifeguards; there are a dozen lifeguard stands along Oceanside's beaches. You can park near the pier along Pacific Street for $0.50 an hour—a bargain, by beach standards. (Not to digress, but just to give an idea of the flavor of life in Oceanside, here's a newsy tidbit from January 2002: "No leads have been developed in the theft of 10 parking meters last week from the downtown area, police said.")

The massive Oceanside Pier is a broad, dark-planked old affair with a devoted fishing clientele. No license is needed to fish off the pier, and a trolley runs to and from it. A community center is attached to the pier in the complex at its base; its gym is open to the public. Just behind the pier sits the **California Surf Museum** (223 North Coast Highway, 760/721-6876), a required stop for people who like people who like beaches.

47 SOUTH OCEANSIDE BEACH

Location: Cassidy and Pacific Streets in Oceanside

Parking/Fees: free street parking
Hours: 24 hours
Facilities: none
Contact: Oceanside Department of Harbors
and Beaches, 760/966-4535

BUCCANEER BEACH

Location: 1506 South Pacific Street in
Oceanside
Parking/Fees: free parking lot
Hours: 24 hours
Facilities: concession, lifeguards, picnic area,
restrooms, and showers
Contact: Oceanside Department of Harbors
and Beaches, 760/435-4005

49 OCEANSIDE BOULEVARD BEACH

Location: Oceanside Boulevard at Pacific
Street in Oceanside
Parking/Fees: free street parking
Hours: 24 hours
Facilities: concession, lifeguards, picnic area,
restrooms, and showers
Contact: Oceanside Department of Harbors
and Beaches, 760/966-4535

50 WISCONSIN STREET BEACH

Location: Wisconsin Street at The Strand in
Oceanside
Parking/Fees: pay parking lot and metered
street parking
Hours: 24 hours
Facilities: lifeguards, restrooms, and showers
Contact: Oceanside Department of Harbors
and Beaches, 760/435-4005

51 TYSON STREET BEACH

Location: Tyson Street at The Strand in
Oceanside

Parking/Fees: metered street parking
Hours: 24 hours
Facilities: concession, lifeguards, picnic area,
restrooms, and showers
Contact: Oceanside Department of Harbors
and Beaches, 760/435-4005

52 PIER VIEW SOUTH

Location: in Oceanside along Pacific Street,
between Witherby Street and the San Luis River
Parking/Fees: metered lot and street parking
Hours: 24 hours
Facilities: concession, lifeguards, restrooms,
showers, and picnic tables
Contact: Oceanside Department of Harbors
and Beaches, 760/435-4005

53 PIER VIEW NORTH

Location: in Oceanside along Pacific Street,
between Witherby Street and the San Luis River
Parking/Fees: metered lot and street parking
Hours: 24 hours
Facilities: concession, lifeguards, restrooms,
showers, and picnic tables
Contact: Oceanside Department of Harbors
and Beaches, 760/435-4005

54 BREAKWATER WAY

Location: in Oceanside at the end of Harbor
Drive, off Pacific Street
Parking/Fees: $5 entrance fee per vehicle
Hours: 24 hours
Facilities: lifeguards, restrooms, and picnic
areas
Contact: Oceanside Department of Harbors
and Beaches, 760/435-4005

55 HARBOR BEACH

Location: in Oceanside at the end of Harbor Drive, off Pacific Street
Parking/Fees: $5 entrance fee per vehicle; RV camping fee $15 per night
Hours: 24 hours
Facilities: lifeguards, restrooms, and picnic areas
Contact: Oceanside Department of Harbors and Beaches, 760/435-4005

56 DEL MAR BEACH (CAMP PENDLETON)

Location: north of Oceanside Harbor, inside Camp Pendleton Military Base
Parking/Fees: free parking lot accessible only to military personnel and their guests
Hours: 8 A.M.-7 P.M. (until 4 P.M. in winter)
Facilities: concession, lifeguards, restrooms, showers, and picnic areas
Contact: Del Mar Lifeguard Station, 760/725-2703

RECREATION AND ATTRACTIONS

- **Bike/Skate Rentals:** El Camino Bike Shop, 121 North El Camino Real, Encinitas, 760/436-2340; Millennial Motors, 505 Mission Avenue, Oceanside, 760/722-2225

- **Boat Cruise:** Helgren's Oceanside Sportfishing, 315 Harbor Drive South, Oceanside, 760/722-2133, www.helgrensportfishing.com

- **Dive Shop:** Pyramid Divers, 282 Harbor Drive South, Oceanside, 760/433-6842

- **Ecotourism:** Buena Vista Audubon Society Nature Center, 2202 South Coast Highway, Oceanside, 760/439-2473

- **Fishing Charters:** Helgren's Oceanside Sportfishing, 315 Harbor Drive South, 760/722-2133

- **Marina:** Oceanside Harbor & Marina, 1540 Harbor Drive, 760/966-4580

- **Pier:** Oceanside Pier, Pacific Street and The Strand, Oceanside, 760/722-5853

- **Rainy Day Attraction:** Mission San Luis Rey, 4050 Mission Avenue, 760/757-3651

- **Shopping/Browsing:** Carlsbad Company Stores, Paseo del Norte, Carlsbad, 760/804-9000

- **Surf Shop:** Action Beach Board Shop, 310 Mission Avenue, Oceanside, 760/722-7101

ACCOMMODATIONS

Oceanside has been sorely lacking in lodgings as inviting as its beaches, but it's begun moving in the right direction. Finally, after years of talk and planning, a contemporary new construction has materialized beside the Oceanside Pier. It's the **Wyndham Oceanside Pier Resort** (333 N. Myers Street, 760/901-1200, $$$), and it opened in 2008. For a posh resort on the California coast, the prices aren't half bad—$118–177 per night for rooms ranging from studios to two-bedroom "condos."

Oceanside Marina Inn (2008 Harbor Drive North, 760/722-1561, www.omihotel.com, $$$) has kitchens and fireplaces to go with its location at Oceanside Harbor. If you're not staying on the harbor, then you're probably best off staying at the **Best Western Oceanside Inn** (1680 Oceanside Boulevard, 760/722-1821, $$), a well-appointed chain motel adjacent to I-5.

COASTAL CUISINE

Meals in Oceanside are grabbed on the run or casually eaten at picnic tables or beach blankets. The surfer theme is mined at the **Longboarder Cafe** (228 North Coast Highway, 760/721-6776, $) and the **Beach Break Cafe** (1902 South Coast Highway, 760/439-6355, $), which serve hearty staples (pancakes, omelets, salads, burgers, burritos) in bright, ocean-themed surroundings. We also like the look of the flash-fried, seafood-filled Baja

Buckets at **Rockin' Baja Coastal Cantina** (258 Harbor Drive South, 760/967-6199, $$), a party-themed bar/restaurant with a franchise on Oceanside Harbor (and only three others in California, so far).

A good, cheap, quick, south-of-the-border-style bite can be had at **Johnny Mañana's** (308 Mission Avenue, 760/721-9999, $). Heaping helpings of fresh, guilt-free Mexican fare are served at low prices in a pleasant, beachy atmosphere. The house special is a BLT burrito, served with guacamole and salsa. It's hard to spend more than five or six bucks here. You can make off with a plain cheese quesadilla and a cold Pacifico beer, served with complimentary salsa and chips, for under $6. The breakfast burrito has jump-started many a surfer's morning.

The oldest restaurant in Oceanside is **101 Cafe** (631 South Coast Highway, 760/722-5220, $), a 1950s-themed flashback to the world of *Happy Days* on Old U.S. 101. The restaurant's origins, in fact, go all the way back to 1928. Stick-to-the-ribs sandwiches, salads, and burgers rule the menu, and time seemingly stands still.

NIGHTLIFE

Oceanside's nightlife can be a bit raw. After a week of sweating in the hills of Camp Pendleton, a marine can work up a profound thirst. To quench it he or she heads into Oceanside, where bar signs offer greetings like "Welcoming Those Who Have Served and Those Serving." Here's a sampling of the cocktail lounges in Oceanside: **Bub's Whiskey Dive** (301 Pier View Way, 760/757-2827), **The Rusty Spur** (406 Pier View Way, 760/722-2216), and **One More That's It Pub** (431 Airport Road, 760/433-3781). Bottom's up!

San Onofre State Beach

The last stop in San Diego County, San Onofre State Beach butts up against the Orange County line. Several things about San Onofre might make some visitors uneasy. First, it sits in the shadow of the San Onofre Nuclear Generating Station, whose twin peaks are visible from the park. Second, San Onofre is surrounded by **Camp Pendleton,** the largest U.S. Marine base in the nation. In fact, the 3,000-acre coastal-canyon park lies on Marine Corps land that has been leased to the state. Camp Pendleton occupies a staggering 250,000 acres, and you never know what might whiz by this deceptively empty landscape. We were enjoying the view from a freeway vista point when an amphibious tank came roaring across the terrain, kicking up dust. We also heard a few jets break the sound barrier. Third, the area is full of rattlesnakes. This is the only venomous snake species found in California, but they sink their fangs into roughly 200 unlucky Southlanders a year. Other snakes native to San Onofre include red racer, gopher, and king. Even so, the most common animal-related injury is the sting of the stingray, which settles in the sand close to shore.

On the positive side, because it lies on a military reservation, San Onofre is gloriously undeveloped. This is what the California coast used to look like way back when—except, of course, for the nuclear power plant.

For more information, contact San Onofre State Park, 949/492-4872, www.parks.ca.gov.

BEACHES

The lengthy stretch of beach at the south end of San Onofre—often referred to as **Bluffs Beach** or simply **San Onofre State Beach**—can be accessed via six numbered trails that descend steeply to it. It is a lengthy beach, with three miles of campsites running along the abandoned stretch of coastal highway (San Onofre Beach Road) above it. At the north end of the campground is a day-use area with parking. There's nothing fancy about **San Onofre Bluffs Campground,** whose 176 sites offer little in the way of shade and can get noisy (thanks to their proximity to

I-5). **San Mateo Campground,** a more recent addition, has 157 sites with electrical and water hookups and lies a mile east of I-5. A mile-long trail leads from this campground to the famed Trestles surfing beach.

San Onofre State Beach is ideal for beginners—"the Waikiki of California," we've seen it called—and surf camps are held along its shores. Want to learn how to surf while camping at San Onofre? Contact Jason Senn at **Endless Summer Surf Camp** (949/498-7862, www.endlesssummersurfcamp.com). This surf expert offers five-day overnight surf camp packages that are often booked solid in the summer months.

Okay, things get a little confusing at this point, so follow closely. Proceeding north from the campground, you encounter San Onofre Nuclear Generating Station (SONGS, of all unlikely acronyms), Old Man's Beach (part of San Onofre State Beach), San Onofre Recreational Beach (which belongs to Camp Pendleton), and Trestles Beach (part of San Onofre State Beach).

Old Man's Beach is a popular spot for older surfers on longboards ("geezers," in surfing lingo). The vibe is mellower than at beaches where adrenalized young surf punks on shortboards carry out their version of *Fight Club* for wave-riding rights. Mexican-style thatched cabanas and volleyball nets add to the festive air.

Next up is **San Onofre Recreational Beach** (a.k.a. Churches Beach), one of two lifeguarded beaches for Camp Pendleton military personnel only. (The other is **Del Mar Beach,** just above Oceanside.)

Rounding out the lineup at San Onofre is **Trestles Beach** ("Trestles," for short, a reference to railroad trestles). Located at San Mateo Point, Trestles offers the best break in San Diego County and one of the best in the continental United States. Trestles is a big reason why so many world-class surfers make their home in nearby San Clemente—and why so many surfers go to the trouble of trotting a half-mile down a pathway with surfboards on their heads to get there.

© PARKE PUTERBAUGH

Trestles Beach

57 BLUFFS BEACH

Location: three miles south of San Clemente via Basilone Road exit off I-5; six bluff-top trails lead to the beach from San Onofre Bluffs Campground
Parking/Fees: $10 entrance fee per vehicle; camping fees are $20-25 per night, plus $7.50 reservation fee
Hours: 6 A.M.-sunset
Facilities: lifeguards, restrooms, showers, and picnic tables
Contact: San Onofre State Beach, 949/492-4872

58 OLD MAN'S BEACH

Location: south of San Clemente via Basilone Road exit off I-5; bluff-top trail leads to beach from north of San Onofre Nuclear Generating Station
Parking/Fees: $10 entrance fee per vehicle
Hours: 6 A.M.-sunset
Facilities: none
Contact: San Onofre State Beach, 949/492-4872

59 SAN ONOFRE RECREATIONAL BEACH (CAMP PENDLETON)

Location: north end of Camp Pendleton, at San Onofre State Beach
Parking/Fees: free parking lot; the lot and beach are accessible only to military personnel and their guests
Hours: 8 A.M.-7 P.M. (until 4 P.M. in winter)
Facilities: concession, lifeguards, restrooms, showers, and picnic areas
Contact: San Onofre Lifeguard Station, 760/725-7935

60 TRESTLES BEACH

Location: accessible by a one-mile hike along path accessed at Christianos Road near I-5 in San Clemente
Parking/Fees: camping fee at San Mateo Campground $29-34 per night with hookup, $20-25 per night without hookup, plus $7.50 reservation fee
Hours: 6 A.M.-sunset
Facilities: none
Contact: San Onofre State Beach, 949/492-4872

MOON SAN DIEGO COUNTY BEACHES

Avalon Travel
a member of the Perseus Books Group
1700 Fourth Street
Berkeley, CA 94710, USA
www.moon.com

Editor: Naomi Adler Dancis
Copy Editor: Kay Elliott
Graphics Coordinator: Kathryn Osgood
Production Coordinators: Amber Pirker,
  Elizabeth Jang
Cover Designer: Kathryn Osgood
Map Editor: Albert Angulo
Cartographers: Jon Twena, Kat Bennett

ISBN-13: 978-1-59880-331-0

Text © 2009 by Alan Bisbort and
Parke Puterbaugh.
Maps © 2009 by Avalon Travel.
All rights reserved.

Front cover photo: Surfing in San Diego
© dreamstime.com
Title page photo: Red succulents near
La Jolla coast © Unclejay/dreamstime.com

Printed in the United States

ABOUT THE AUTHORS

Alan Bisbort

Alan Bisbort is a writer, editor, and researcher who has authored or coauthored nearly 20 books of history, biography, travel, and poetry, and contributed to numerous other books. He has worked for the Library of Congress, on staff or on contract, since 1977. As a freelance journalist, he is a regular contributor to *The New York Times*, the *Hartford, Valley Advocates, Yale Environment Journal, Yale Medicine, Connecticut, American Politics Journal, AMP*, and *Ugly Things*. His work has also appeared in *The Washington Post, Rolling Stone, American Way, Los Angeles Times, City Paper, Creem, Biblio*, and *Washingtonian*.

Though Alan lives on the East Coast, he has spent a great deal of time in California over the past ten years, researching four editions of *Moon California Beaches* with Parke Puterbaugh. Since high school he has been guilty of unrepentant California dreaming. Alan lives near New Haven, Connecticut with his wife, award-winning journalist Tracey O'Shaughnessy, their son, Paul James, and their ageless dog, Sam.

Parke Puterbaugh

Parke Puterbaugh is a writer, editor, and educator who mainly works in the music and travel fields. A rock-music enthusiast and scholar, he is a former senior editor for *Rolling Stone* magazine. After nearly a decade in New York City, he longed to work in more natural surroundings, and the idea of writing beach guidebooks – inspired by a lifelong love of coastal environments – came to him. The publication of *Moon California Beaches* coincides with the 25th anniversary of his and Alan's decision to ditch their respective jobs to embark on lives of itinerant beachcombing and full-time freelancing. They have written several celebrated beach guidebooks, and have visited every public beach in the continental U.S. that can be reached by car, foot, or ferry.

Parke further pursued his interest in beaches and barrier islands in the classroom. He earned a master's degree in environmental science, with emphases in coastal geology and coastal-zone management, from the University of North Carolina at Chapel Hill. He has written a guide to Southeastern wetlands for the U.S. Environmental Protection Agency, as well as several music-related titles, including a forthcoming biography of the rock group Phish. Parke's work has also been published in more than 30 magazines and newspapers. He has served as a freelance writer, historian, and curatorial consultant for the Rock and Roll Hall of Fame and Museum since its inception. Presently, he teaches in the music department at Guilford College in Greensboro, North Carolina, where he lives with his wife, Carol, and daughter, Hayley.